Toward a Theology of Nature

Essays on Science and Faith

Wolfhart Pannenberg

Edited by Ted Peters

Westminster/John Knox Press
Louisville, Kentucky

Book design by Drew Stevens
Cover design: Susan E. Jackson
Cover art: Pleiades. Oil painting by Cecilia Amorocho, 1993.

First edition

Published by Westminster/John Knox Press
Louisville, Kentucky

This book is printed on acid-free paper that meets the American National Standards Institute Z39.48 standard. ∞

PRINTED IN THE UNITED STATES OF AMERICA
9 8 7 6 5 4 3 2 1

Library of Congress Cataloging-in-Publication Data

Pannenberg, Wolfhart
    Toward a theology of nature : essays on science and faith /
Wolfhart Pannenberg : edited by Ted Peters.
        p.   cm.
    Includes index.
    ISBN 0-664-25384-9 (pbk. : alk. paper)

    1. Nature—Religious aspects—Christianity.   Religion and
science. 3. Creation. 4. Natural law. 5. Physics—Religious
aspects—Christianity. I. Peters, Ted, 1941–   . II. Title.
BT695.5.P36   1993
261.5'5—dc20   93-19480

Lead me in your truth, and teach me,
for you are the God of my salvation;
for you I wait all day long.

—*Psalm 25:5*

Contents

Acknowledgments

"Theological Questions to Scientists" was previously published in *Zygon* 16:1 (March 1981): 65–76, and in the *CTNS Bulletin* 7:2 (Spring 1987). Used by permission of Blackwell Publishers, Oxford.

"The Doctrine of Creation and Modern Science" appeared in *Cosmos as Creation: Theology and Science in Consonance*, copyright © 1989 Abingdon Press; ed. Ted Peters (Nashville: Abingdon Press, 1989), 152–76. Reprinted by permission. Another version of this essay was published in *Zygon* 23:1 (March 1988): 3–21, and in *The CTNS Bulletin* 7:2 (Spring 1987): 1–10.

"God and Nature" appeared originally as "Gott und die Natur" in *Theologie und Philosophie* 58 (1983): 481–500. Wilhelm C. Linss is the translator.

"Contingency and Natural Law" appeared originally as "Kotingenz und Naturgesetz" in *Erwägungen zu einer Theologie der Natur*, by A. M. Klaus Müller and Wolfhart Pannenberg (Gütersloh: Verlagshaus Gerd Mohn, 1970), 33–80. Wilhelm C. Linss is the translator.

"The Doctrine of the Spirit and the Task of a Theology of Nature" was published in *Theology* 75:1 (1972): 8–20. Used by permission of SPCK, London, publisher.

"Spirit and Energy" appeared originally as "Geist und Energie: Zur Phänomenologie Teilhards de Chardin," *Acta Teilhardiana* 8 (1971): 5–12. Donald K. Musser is the translator with help from David Strobel.

Acknowledgments

"Spirit and Mind" appeared in *Mind and Nature* (Gustavus Adolphus College Nobel Conference XVII), copyright © 1982 by Gustavus Adolphus College; Richard Q. Elvee (San Francisco: Harper & Row, 1982), 134–57.

A special note of gratitude is offered to Philip Hefner and the Chicago Center for Religion and Science for their cooperation in producing this English-language collection of Pannenberg's writings, especially for their aid in securing the translations by Wilhelm Linss and Donald Musser. In November 1988 the Chicago Center for Religion and Science sponsored an international symposium intended to lead to a volume of published papers that will complement this one. It will be co-edited by Carol Rausch Albright and Joel Haugen, with the tentative title *Laying Theological Claim to Scientific Understanding: Pannenberg in Dialogue with Scientists.*

Pannenberg on Theology and Natural Science

Perhaps the most startling and dramatic contribution of Wolfhart Pannenberg to recent theological discussion has been the initiative he takes in posing theological questions to natural scientists. Whereas most of the religious community timidly seeks ways to incorporate the worldview of twentieth-century physics and biology by adjusting the religious vision accordingly, Pannenberg has reversed the process. Rather than simply respond to scientific theories as if they come to us prepackaged and complete, the Munich theologian criticizes the scientific vision of nature as incomplete; and he proceeds to challenge scientists to consider incorporating the idea of God into the picture they paint. Unless God is properly considered, he argues, a scientific theory cannot fully comprehend the reality of the world it seeks to explain. The natural world is a creature of a creating God, and unless this is understood, the natural world itself cannot be understood.

It may seem as though Pannenberg is violating something sacred. Since the rise of the so-called "two cultures," the Western mind has tacitly dubbed the scientific to be "holy" and the religious to be "profane." We have come to assume that scientific knowledge is pure, whereas so-called religious knowledge is profaned by subjective feeling or atavistic superstition. We have come to assume that scientific research needs to be rational and empirical and that religious sentiments contaminate our understanding of nature with unfounded prejudices regarding the unprovable reality of God. Academic freedom seems to require the exclusion of theology from the temple of scientific knowing. Rather than violate this taboo, theologians for the last century or so have trod lightly on questions regarding God and the natural world, ceding to the scientific community the priestly right to dispense the graces of understanding nature. Now, however, Pannenberg seems to be profaning what Western Enlightenment culture has held sacred. He is brashly reentering the epistemological holy of holies and contending that loss of an awareness of God actually constricts what we learn about the nature of nature. The stakes are high for those scientists who take Pannenberg's challenge to heart. It means a return to the laboratory with a reassessment of the meaning of existing evidence and a posing of new questions for future research.

The stakes are high for theologians as well. Up until now, theologians have made themselves feel reasonably secure by hiding behind the Kantian split between theoretical and moral knowledge and by consigning science to the former while reserving privileged access to the latter. Even if natural scientists exclude God from their worldview, theologians have thought they could earn an honest living by appealing to the realm of value and morality. No longer, says Pannenberg. In the first chapter of this collection of essays, Pannenberg makes it clear that the challenge goes both ways: "If the God of the Bible is the creator of the universe, then it is not possible to understand fully or even appropriately the processes of nature without any reference to that God. If, on the contrary, nature can be appropriately understood without reference to the God of the Bible, then that God cannot be the creator of the universe, and consequently he cannot be truly God and be trusted as a source of moral teaching either." If we fail to make the case that the God in whom Christians place their faith is also the God of created nature, then we can claim no privileged access to God through ethics. The former is the foundation of the latter.

This is significant in at least three ways. First, Pannenberg is raising the current dialogue between theologians and natural scientists to a new level of seriousness. Second, he asks us to think of theology as scientific in character and, hence, sharing at least in part the same method and even domain as the natural sciences. Third, he is challenging us to develop a theology of nature that relies on both modern science and classical Christian commitments regarding creation, conservation, and governance. In the seven previously published essays included here in this volume, Pannenberg's theology of nature will be clearly developed. In this introduction, I would like to draw out the significance of the Pannenberg challenge for the interchange between theologians and scientists and then outline briefly the direction that Pannenberg's scientific theology of nature is taking.

Pannenberg and the Dialogue
Between Theology and Natural Science

Where does Pannenberg fit in the current dialogue among theologians and scientists? Just asking about the dialogue between theologians and scientists, of course, presupposes that healthy conversation is taking place. It is. But it has not always been this way.

Since the consolidation of the natural sciences in Western universities following the Enlightenment, we have been playing a kind of intellectual volleyball. On the one side we have encountered *scientism*, sometimes known as "naturalism" or "secular humanism." Scientism claims total victory on the grounds that science is the sole course of trustworthy knowledge. There is only one reality, the natural world, and experimental science provides the only trusted methods for learning the truth about this reality. Religion, in contrast, provides no knowledge. The best it can do is create fictions about nonexistent realities. Thus, what the theologians say is only pseudo-knowledge, not the real thing.

On the other side of the net we find the competition, usually one or another form of religious *authoritarianism*. The players on this team assume that special revelation constitutes the highest truth. What we learn from the laboratory or from natural reason, then, must be subject to evaluation from the point of view of faith. Authoritarianism has two strings of players, the ecclesiastical and the biblical. According to ecclesiastical authoritarianism, a good example of which is the 1864 *Syllabus of Errors* promulgated by Pope Pius IX, it is an error to think that science or philosophy should withdraw from supervision by the higher discipline of theology. In the event that natural methods of gaining knowledge produce a conclusion that contradicts what we believe theologically, then we must assert that theology is right and the other is wrong. Because the church knows the revealed truth, it has the right to direct the course that the sciences take. In a similar fashion, Protestant fundamentalists fight for a biblical version of authoritarianism, relying on special revelation as it is found in the text of the Bible. Because the book of Genesis seems to say that God fixed the species during the seven-day creation, fundamentalists deny truth value to scientific claims that one species evolved from another through mutation over long periods of time. In short, authority defeats theory.

Waiting on the sideline for their turn to play as substitutes for the fundamentalists we can see the *scientific creationists*. Their strategy is different. Whereas the fundamentalists of the 1920s had relied on the authority of the Bible on the grounds that it is divinely inspired, today's scientific creationists are willing to play their game in the scientists' court. They assume that revealed knowledge and scientific knowledge belong to the same domain, so they must harmonize. When a dispute arises between a scientific claim and a religious claim, what we have is a dispute between rival scientific theories. This means that the biblical account of the seven-day creation is in fact a scientific theory, subject to confirmation by geological and biological evidence. Just because of this evidence, they claim, the Genesis account is superior to its rival: the theory of evolution. This is a nonauthoritarian approach to faith, and, whether they win or lose, creationists declare that they want to play the game according to the same rules by which the scientists play.

What we would expect to find is a hotly contested game between the established natural scientists on one side, and, on the other side, any one of the three: the ecclesiastical authoritarians, the fundamentalist authoritarians, or the scientific creationists. What we would expect to find is a spirited match to settle the matter, to see who wins and who loses. Surprisingly, however, twentieth-century watchers have seen very little competitive volleying across the net. Why? Because the majority of players on both sides have adopted the *two-language rule*. According to the two-language theory, scientists and theologians work in separate domains of knowledge, speak separate languages, and, when true to their respective disciplines, avoid interfering in each other's work. What we end up with are two teams, each sparring with its own volleyball on its respective side of the net. If the creationists who reject the two-language rule serve the ball into the scientists' court, the scientists do not bother to return it. But when the players of the fourth string made up of liberal or neo-orthodox theologians take the religious side of the court, they tout the two-language rule and send nothing over the net. This has kept the scientific team happy for most of the present century.

The two-language theory has eliminated the competition. Proffered primarily by the liberal and neo-orthodox theologians, this theory holds that there is no connection whatsoever between what Christians believe about God's creation of the universe and the observable creation that is the result. This is because the theologians and scientists allegedly ask different questions. Scientists ask about objective knowledge that deals with this world, whereas theologians ask about existential or personal knowledge that deals with our relation to what transcends this world. Scientists ask *how?* Theologians ask *why?* Scientists deal with fact, whereas theologians deal with value. Scientists search for proximate causes, whereas theologians search for ultimate origins. What this split in languages permits, of course, is for each of us to be bilingual—that is, to pursue both science and faith without conflict.

The two-language game is played by scientists as well as by theologians. In a 1939 address on "Science and Religion," noted physicist Albert Einstein distinguished between the language of fact and the language of value. "Science can only ascertain what *is*," he said, "but not what *should be*. Religion, on the other hand, deals only with evaluations of human thought and action." Significant in Einstein's remark here is the word "only," because it signifies that each language is restricted to its own domain. Those who speak for religion may speak of value, not fact.

Over the last decade, the tenor of the game has been gradually changing as the two-language rule gives way to an emerging approach, *hypothetical consonance*. In contrast to the two-language separatists, those searching for consonance assume that both science and theology share some domains of knowing. Scientific knowledge of the natural world, for example, is knowledge about that which God has created. There is but one reality, a creaturely reality created by a creator God. Hypothetically, knowledge gained about the natural world should contribute to what we know about God, and, conversely, what we know about God should influence how we understand the natural world. The task now is to explore the various disciplines looking for possible crossovers, commonalties, and complementarities. This task gives us a reason to put open-minded scientists and working theologians into conversation with one another. Hypothetical consonance does not return us to a win-lose competition, but it does suggest tentative volleys across the net to see how the other side plays them.

The growing dissatisfaction with the two-language theory and the increasing sense that there must be some areas of possible consonance are actually producing good-natured volleying between scientists and theologians. Physicists and biologists have been meeting with dogmaticians and ethicists in an attempt to sort out issues of methodology, conceptuality, and morality. Centers for ongoing research are coming into existence and hosting dialogues with increasing frequency and growing sophistication. In Germany, we note the leadership of Hans May and the work of the Evangelische

Akademie Loccum. The Vatican Observatory near Rome sponsors serious investigations into scientific matters because the pope, John Paul II, deems it important. In England, Arthur Peacocke has organized the Society of Ordained Scientists. At Princeton, we find the Center of Theological Inquiry and the scholarship of Wentzel van Huyssteen. In Chicago, Philip Hefner heads the Center for Religion and Science. In Berkeley, research conferences and dialogues are sponsored by the Center for Theology and the Natural Sciences directed by Robert John Russell. Lutherans, Presbyterians, and the United Church of Christ support task forces on science and technology. Gustavus Adolphus College holds biennial convocations that put Nobel Prize-winning scientists into conversation with theologians. Although no new worldview has yet emerged from these discussions, scholars from various fields press on with the conversations because they sense the possible widening of horizons for all concerned. Although scientists and theologians still speak two languages, to be sure, what we find today is an earnest desire to communicate.

This is the world setting within which Wolfhart Pannenberg asks how theology might become more scientific and how science might become more theological. As one of the most serious participants in these dialogues, Pannenberg exploits the interdisciplinary setting because he listens to what scientists say; and he also takes the initiative to say things to scientists.

Theology as the Science of God

Up to now Pannenberg's major scholarly contribution to the science-theology dialogue has been the publication (1973 in German and 1976 in English) of his *Theology and the Philosophy of Science*. We must think of theology as scientific (*wissenschaftlich*), Pannenberg argues, because it employs the same method as that found in the sciences, and in addition theology deals at least in part with the same finite reality. He wants to extricate theology from its self-imposed isolation, to extract it from its ghetto and place it in the arena of open discussion with other disciplines. Theology asks about the truth of Christian claims, and we cannot inquire into the truth about Christianity without also inquiring into the question of the truth of all areas of human experience.

In *Theology and the Philosophy of Science*, Pannenberg offers a commentary and critique of the groundbreaking new insights of post–World War II philosophers of science, insights into the sociology of knowledge and such that have served to open conversation between the two languages. Through this analysis and critique, Pannenberg hopes to put a gate in the wall that has divided the two cultures, the *Naturwissenschaften* and the *Geisteswissenschaften*. That gate swings on the hinges of meaning. Whether in the natural sciences or the humanities, interpreters of reality find themselves working intersubjectively in a context of meaning, a context conditioned by one's semantic network and wider cultural setting. That context is both transcendent yet immanent to the individual. The context-individual dialectic becomes a whole-part dialectic. Moving beyond the now sterile mind-body dualism of Descartes, Pannenberg appeals to systems theory and similar modes of thinking to cultivate awareness of the systematic dependency of bits of meaning on their wider context.

The greatest contribution to our understanding of meaning, however, comes to us from hermeneutical philosophers such as Wilhelm Dilthey, Hans-Georg Gadamer, and Jürgen Habermas. These hermeneuts recognize that all experience of meaning anticipates by implication the widest possible context of meaning—that is, the whole of reality. God is the correlate to the whole of humanity. The idea of God—defined as the all-determining reality—becomes the hypothesis raised by Pannenberg to provide the most adequate explanation for the experience of meaning.

Because God is thought of as the all-determining reality, and because the divine presence is known through the experience of meaning, Pannenberg asserts that theology itself incorporates the scientific domain and method. It incorporates the scientific domain because theology is a field-encompassing field. There is no corner of the real world that is outside the field of theological investigation. As theology investigates with scientific method, it ought not to claim any privileged status for its faith assertions. The task of theology is to examine the thesis of faith as a hypothesis. The hypothesis of faith must be either true or false, and the task of the theologian is to explore the possibility of its truth. In doing so, theology ought not to claim a field of investigation that is separated or isolated from others.

Does this make theology empirical? No, not exactly. Although it may consider everything it studies in relation to the reality of God it posits, in itself theology is not a positive science engaged in empirical experimentation. It is, rather, a reflective discipline, drawing out implications of positive knowledge for an intelligible picture of the whole. What sharply distinguishes theology from the focused work of empirical research is its comprehensive scope. The investigation of God as the all-determining reality involves the whole of reality, and broad reflection on the connections of empirically derived data is the method for getting at the whole.

With what we have just said as a foundation, Pannenberg erects a theology understood as the "science of God." If theology is to be scientific and to propose hypotheses, then it cannot sidestep the problem of verification. Pannenberg contends that each theological assertion has the logical structure of a hypothesis; therefore it is subject to verification against the relevant state of affairs it seeks to explain. But how does one confirm or disconfirm an assertion about God? Theology cannot follow a method of direct verification, because the existence of its object, God, is itself in dispute and because God—as the all-determining reality—is not a reproducible finite entity. An indirect method of verification is available, however. Influenced in part by Karl Popper's procedures for critical verification and falsification, Pannenberg says that we can test assertions by their implications. Assertions about a divine life and divine actions can be tested by their implications for understanding the whole of finite reality, a wholeness that is implicitly anticipated in the ordinary experience of meaning.

Because of the temporal process in which the finite world is ever changing, the whole, which is an essential framework for any item of experience to have a determinate meaning, does not exist at any point as a totality. Rather, it can only be imagined by transcending what exists at any point in time. Thus the anticipation, without which no meaningful experience is possible at all, always involves an element of hypothesis that must be confirmed or refuted by subsequent experience. Even the reality of God fits into this class. The reality of God is present to us now only in subjective anticipation of the totality of finite reality, in a conceptual model of the whole of meaning presupposed in all particular experience. Such a model— for example, the idea of the eschatological kingdom of God that arises from our historic religious tradition—is subject to future confirmation or refutation by what happens. It is this openness to confirmation that makes theological assertions hypothetical and, hence, scientific.

The anticipation of wholeness of meaning within common human experience is the key that makes Pannenberg's method work. We anticipate a wholeness of meaning that is not yet fully present, a wholeness that we hypothesize will come in the future as the gift of an eschatological act of the one God. The *direct confirmation* of this hypothesis is dependent on the actual coming of that eschatological wholeness. In the meantime, while we await the eschatological fulfillment, the faith hypothesis can gain *indirect confirmation* by the increased intelligibility it offers to our understanding of our experience of finite reality. If in fact God is the all-determining reality, then everything else we study, including the natural world, must eventually be shown to be determined by this reality. The very raising of the hypothesis of God as the all-determining one can be evaluated positively if it increases the intelligibility of the natural world by considering it in relation to God that places Pannenberg in dialogue with scientists and leads him toward a theology of nature.

Toward a Theology of Nature

One of the areas of physical cosmology that needs increased intelligibility, according to Pannenberg in the chapters of the present book, is the relationship between natural law and the contingency of individual events. An event is contingent if a description of it is neither self-evident nor necessary, if it could have happened differently. Here we run into a problem of focus in the scientific community, because virtually all the theoretical attention is given to the regularity of nature's laws, while the contingency of natural events slips into the nearly invisible background. What researchers concentrate on are the uniformities that can be expressed in timeless equations. A dictionary of equations describing these uniformities allegedly constitutes scientific knowledge.

A closer examination, however, reveals that the applicability of these equations to concrete cases of natural processes requires certain initial and marginal conditions, conditions that in every case are contingent. Only when contingent conditions permit can we expect a natural law to operate as expected. Pannenberg observes that statements of natural law necessarily presuppose their material as contingently given. This fact is hidden, because the scientific formulas themselves ignore their respective contexts of contingency while concentrating their attention on the uniformities that occur in natural phenomena. Although the contingency of individual events is assumed, what comes to thematization are the laws. If we focus only on the laws, we draw the mistaken conclusion that the actual course of events is utterly determined by these laws. Determinacy gets thematized, whereas contingency gets ignored. Also, because God's actions cannot be put in an equation or formulated as a natural law, the study of nature cannot help becoming deistic or atheistic. In sum, what we think of as nature's laws are actually abstract principles drawn from the more concrete course of contingent natural events. This means that our dictionary of natural laws cannot possibly provide an exhaustive description of natural processes.

This means further that nature ought to be understood as historical. Why? If what we take to be natural laws are uniformities abstracted from the actual course of contingent events, then each event is temporally unique. This implies, Pannenberg argues in the second volume of his *Systematic Theology*, an irreversibility to time (*Unumkehrbarkeit der Zeit*). Even if the laws of classical dynamics are in principle temporally reversible, the actual course of natural events from which those laws have been abstracted is not. The reality of nature is first and foremost a historical reality.

Pannenberg should be gratified by recent discussions of thermodynamics that seem to compel the scientific community to embrace the irreversibility of time. At least one friendly critic, physicist and theologian Robert John Russell, chides Pannenberg for not pressing his case further into physical cosmology. Not only would thermodynamics seem to support Pannenberg's notion of the historicity of the cosmos, but the anthropic principle, according to which contingent events seem to be directed toward the creation of life as we know it, could also be garnered by the Munich theologian for support.

Be that as it may, what Pannenberg capitalizes on is this recognition that nature has an essential historical dimension, because history may provide the open gate that will permit increased traffic between the scientific side and the theological side of the fence. Theologians are at home in history. God acts. And God's acts have historical effects, and such effects can be apprehended only as contingently and temporally unique. Theology can be understood as the study of the history of God's activity. So, what Pannenberg is trying to do is to move the scientist from a focus on the abstracted uniformities of nature to the presupposed background of nature's contingent course of events; and this should open up the possibility of dialogue with the theologian on common ground.

To the theologian, the enduring forms of nature right along with single events appear as the contingent product of the activity of a free God. The very existence of the world in the first place is the result of a free and loving act by God; and the uniformities of nature which endure through time are the result of God's continuing and faithful attention to the world. Although God's acts are contingent and underivable from any higher principle, they maintain continuity with previous divine actions while opening the future to as yet unforeseeable actions.

Creation, Conservation, and Governance

In his *Systematic Theology* and in the essays of this book, we will see that Pannenberg approaches these concerns through the theological categories of creation (*Schöpfung, creatio*), conservation (*Erhaltung, conservatio*), and governance (*Regierung, gubernatio*). Beginning with the category of creation, he notes that the very existence of the world is itself contingent. No law of nature requires that the world exist. It might not have existed. Yet it does. Any regularity within nature presupposes the existence of nature as brutely given. Theologians attempt to explain this with the doctrine of *creatio ex nihilo*, creation out of nothing, which claims that a totally free God created this world apart from any forces external to that God's loving desire to bring such a world into existence.

In regard to the category of conservation, Pannenberg argues that God's action in the world continues even though the world itself is already established. Closely tied to the origin of creation is the conservation of the creation. He is no deist. He is a theist, indicating that he believes that the continued existence of the world is sustained by God's continued care for it. And its sustained existence is characterized both by uniform laws of nature and by the course of contingent events, living events. The creation does not remain what it was at its point of origin. It changes. It develops. New forms appear. New things happen. There is a sense in which one can say that *creatio ex nihilo* is complemented by *creatio continua*, continuing creation.

Turning finally to the category of governance, we have to ask about the purpose or goal of created nature. Pannenberg does not belong to that school of philosophers who believe there is an innate *telos* or entelechy that is directing the course of natural evolution toward a sublime goal. Yet what happens is not without purpose. This purpose comes from God's governance, that providential activity aimed at accomplishing the divinely appointed end.

Pannenberg asks: What is this purpose? Is the full appreciation God in the Godself (the *visio Dei*) the end and goal, as Thomas Aquinas has suggested? No, this cannot be it. Or is the purpose of created nature to glorify and praise God, as the early Protestants contended? No, not this either. To say that God in the Godself or the glory of God or such is the final goal to which all of nature is directed is to make God look like a divine narcissist and to neglect a very important tenet of Christian theology, namely, God created the world out of love. The created world is an object of God's love. God's purpose for created nature has to do with created nature, with its own creaturely fulfillment. The purpose of nature comes external to nature, from God; but it is a purpose *for* nature.

The concept of governance implies resistance. The created world, according to the Christian understanding, is independent of God. It is not an emanation or extension of the divine being. It is distinct. It is an object of God's love, not an extension of God's self-love. As independent, the created world has the freedom to depart from God's purposes. It does. The presence of sin and evil indicates this. Hence, the governance of God is expressed through the continued divine activity which seeks to transform evil into good; it is the work of redemption. Creation is complemented by redemption.

The direction in which this divine governance is taking us can be discerned by looking at the event of the *logos* incarnate in Jesus of Nazareth and the vision of the eschatological kingdom of God. It is fascinating to note that Pannenberg places the eternal *logos* not in the category of uniform laws of nature but rather in that of contingent events. The *logos* is not the abstract but the concrete order of the created world. The *logos* is not a timeless structure; rather, it is the actual historically derived principle by which the created world will attain its unity and fulfillment.

The event of incarnation and the idea of the *logos* are not at odds with each other. The function of the *logos* is not that of abstract description but rather a concrete creative principle. The incarnation is the center for the integration of the historical order of the world, which will attain its world-unifying actualization and fulfillment with the arrival of the eschatological kingdom of God. Rightly understood, the incarnation is no mere ornamental addition to the creation. It is not merely the reaction of the creator to Adam's fall into sin. Much more, the incarnation is the signpost pointing to the future City of God as the end or purpose toward which all of God's creative and conserving activity has been directed.

The idea of the faithfulness of God binds together the notions of conservation and governance with that of contingent creation. This indicates theologically that God is by no means static or that the created order is made up of eternally fixed forms, as previous theologians may have mistakenly thought; rather, the faithfulness of the creating God continues to conserve the existence of this world while drawing it forward toward a new and transformed state of existence. This faithfulness to the world on the part of God is something that Christians in particular can appreciate, because, according to the Christian doctrine of the Trinity, that faithfulness already characterizes the relationship between Father, Son, and Holy Spirit. God's creating and sustaining love for the world is an extension of that love which is already internal to the divine life.

A Field Theory of Spirit

The relationship between uniform laws of nature and the contingency of particular events provides the formal point of departure for Pannenberg's theological analysis of modern science. What remains is the material content of scientific theorizing and the description of reality that emerges. One area to which he has devoted considerable attention is the concept of the force field in physics. The work of Michael Faraday and his successors such as Albert Einstein draws particular interest. The achievement of the field concept is that it reverses the previous view that forces are solely the unmediated result of bodies in motion, that action-at-a-distance is precluded. To Faraday, in contrast, the body is a manifestation of force field; and a force field is an independent reality prior to the body. Body and mass become secondary phenomena, concentrations of dynamic force at particular places and points in the field. Action-at-a-distance is possible.

This is theologically significant for a number of reasons. First, the problem with the post-Newtonian reduction of forces to mass in motion is that the resulting picture of the universe precludes any divine force. If God does not have a body, and if all forces require a prior body, then God cannot have force. This problem is eliminated with contemporary field theory.

This is theologically significant for a second reason. Dynamic field theories from Faraday to Einstein claim a priority for the whole over the parts. The value of this is that God and the whole are correlate categories. God, as the all-determining reality, must be conceived to be the unifying ground of the whole universe if the divine is to be conceived as creator and redeemer of the world. By appealing to the divinely granted whole of reality, Pannenberg believes he can make the effective presence of God in every single contingent event intelligible. To increase this intelligibility, Pannenberg points out that the field concept was originally a metaphysical concept going back to the pre-Socratics. By the time the Stoics got a hold of it, the field had become associated with the *pneuma*, the divine Spirit.

This brings us to the third reason that field theory in physics is theologically significant: it provides a possible means for conceiving of the divine Spirit as active in the natural world. Even more—and this may be one of the most courageous of his conceptual hypotheses—Pannenberg employs the notion of a dynamic field to describe the workings of the Spirit within the trinitarian life proper. The essence of divinity is spirit, he says; and it is due to the Holy Spirit *as a dynamic force field* that the Son is generated from the Father and that the two, the Father and the Son, are bound together in love. The Holy Spirit is the love that generates the Son, creates the cosmos, precipitates redemption, and unifies all. The persons of the trinitarian Godhead and the independent creation are singularities arising from the dynamic field of the Spirit's activity.

Pannenberg rushes in where two-language angels have feared to tread. He does not say that spirit *is like* a force field. He says spirit *is* a force field. There is a directness and a literalness here that seems to throw caution to the wind. One can admire his scholarly courage, but perhaps this assertion should retain its hypothetical status for a period to await confirmation or disconfirmation. Historians of science are quick to point out the dangers of trying to float a theological assertion aboard a scientific ship, because the intellectual weather can change suddenly. New discoveries and new theories have repeatedly whipped up the winds of change, and new waves of thought have again and again swamped and sunk previously held scientific ideas. How long will field theory stay afloat? If someday it should sink, will Pannenberg's theology of spirit sink with it?

The relationship between field theory and spirit is by no means the only scientific topic to which Pannenberg responds. He exerts similar energy to analyze and reconceptualize the relationship between temporality and eternity in response to physical cosmology; and he tries to offer help in interpreting emergent evolution by invoking an understanding of God as a source of newness. These are exercises that show the doctrinal directions that his methodological commitments would take us. He is committed to showing that only when this natural world is understood as the creation of the biblical God can we test the truth claims of the Christian faith. Only under this presupposition can we posit that the historical event of Jesus Christ is redemptively effective and that we have grounds for hope in its eschatological completion in the kingdom of God. It is this very claim that compels Christian theologians to seek out dialogue with scientists trying to understand the natural world in which we live.

TED PETERS

Pacific Lutheran Theological Seminary
and the Center for Theology and the Natural Sciences
at the Graduate Theological Union, Berkeley, California
On Galileo's 329th birthday, February 15, 1993

1

Theological Questions
to Scientists

In their discussions with theologians few scientists seem motivated primarily by theoretical questions. There is rarely much desire for theologians' help in explaining the world of nature. Rather, there is a widespread awareness that science alone cannot cope with the consequences and side effects of scientific discoveries, especially in their technological application. Frightened earlier by the development of nuclear weapons and later by the threat of ecological disaster and by the dangers involved in modern biochemical techniques, many scientists have been led by a sense of responsibility for the application of their work to look for moral resources that can be mustered in order to prevent or at least to reduce the extent of fatal abuse of the possibilities provided by scientific discoveries. At this point, then, the churches are appreciated once more as moral agencies that should help the human society in responsibly dealing with the potential of science and technology.

The churches should certainly not refuse to face their particular responsibilities in these matters, and theology may be of some assistance here. But in modern society the moral authority of the churches and their theologies is limited. It has been seriously weakened because the underlying religious interpretation of reality is taken no longer as universally valid but as a matter of private preference, if not as superstition.

This situation has been brought about not primarily perhaps but to a large extent by what has been called the "warfare" of science with theology. According to public opinion in our Western culture, this war was lost by Christian apologetics. This does not necessarily mean that the issues have been solved to everyone's satisfaction. On the side of Christian theology a lot of bad apologetics was certainly involved, especially in the long struggle against the principles of continuity and evolution in natural processes. But there were also important issues at stake. On the side of scientific culture a sort of overkill was achieved when scientific inquiry was declared independent of any association with religion. That amounted of course to denying religion its claim on the reality of nature.

It was little comfort in this situation that some religious interpretation of the findings of science was regarded as compatible with science in terms of a private and optional belief. Scientists personally continuing to hold and develop religious views of their work did not alter the fact that, concerning human knowledge of the natural world, religious assertions were considered superfluous. Religion did not make any difference to the scientific description of the reality of nature, and the logical implication was that it had no legitimate claim on reality; the reality of nature could be fully understood without the God of religious faith. In view of the seriousness of this blow to religious truth claims, it would seem appropriate if the renewed interest of scientists in religion and especially in a dialogue with Christian theology were accompanied by some sense of surprise that Christianity is still around. Perhaps Christianity survived only by temporarily separating the outlook of faith from the rational and scientific investigation and description of the natural world. But such an attitude cannot persist, because it is profoundly unacceptable on theological grounds.

If the God of the Bible is the creator of the universe, then it is not possible to understand fully or even appropriately the processes of nature without any reference to that God. If, on the contrary, nature can be appropriately understood without reference to the God of the Bible, then that God cannot be the creator of the universe, and consequently he cannot be truly God and be trusted as a source of moral teaching either. To be sure, the reality of God is not incompatible with some form of abstract knowledge concerning the regularities of natural processes, a knowledge that abstracts from the concreteness of physical reality and therefore may be able also to abstract from the presence of God in his creation. But such abstract knowledge of regularities should not claim full and exclusive competence regarding the explanation of nature; if it does so, the reality of God is denied by implication. The so-called methodological atheism of modern science is far from pure innocence. It is a highly ambiguous phenomenon. Yet its very possibility can be regarded as based on the unfailing faithfulness of the creator God to the creation, providing it with the unviolable regularities of natural processes that themselves become the basis of individual and more precarious and transitory natural systems—from stars and mountains and valleys and oceans to the wonders of plants and animal life, resulting in the rise of the human species.

The abstract investigation of the regularities underlying the emergence of these natural forms need not separate them from their natural context in the creation of God and thus from God himself. But in fact there has been a strong tendency in modern science toward such a separation by subjecting the knowledge of the abstract regularities of nature to human use for human purposes. Precisely the abstract character of modern sciences allows the results to be at the disposal of human groups and societies and to serve the most diverse aims. Using scientific research for ever-extended domination and exploitation of natural resources has deeply influenced the direction of research itself. Modern experimental science not simply observes the natural processes but invades them. Thus it does not leave the change of the natural environment to technological application but starts itself on that line by its experimental techniques.

That modern science so easily lends itself to abuse cannot be prevented in principle. It is one of the risks involved in the abstract study of the regularities that either are inherent in nature itself or can be imposed on natural processes. This risk cannot be met on the level of scientific description itself but must be met first on the level of philosophical reflection on the work of science. It is on this level that the abstract form of scientific description must be considered with special attention to what it is "abstracted from" and what is methodically disregarded in the abstract formulas of science. It is on this level, then, that theologians should address their questions to scientists, since God the creator and the nature of things as creatures belong to those aspects of reality which are abstracted from in the mathematical language of science.

There are five such questions that will be raised in the rest of this chapter. They have been selected because all of them seem to be of particular importance in the dialogue between natural science and theology. The answers given to each of these questions will contribute significantly to any decision concerning the compatibility of modern science with faith in the biblical God as creator and redeemer of humankind and of the entire creation.

The first and most fundamental of these questions runs like this: Is it conceivable, in view of the importance of contingency in natural processes, to revise the principal of inertia or at least its interpretation? The introduction of this principle in modern science played a major role in depriving God of his function in the conservation of nature and in finally rendering him an unnecessary hypothesis in the understanding of natural processes. Closely connected is the second question: Is the reality of nature to be understood as contingent, and are natural processes to be understood as irreversible? This question aims at the historical character of reality—not only of human history but also of nature—that seems to be specifically related to the biblical idea of God.

The third question is related also to the biblical perspectives of created existence and especially of life: Is there any equivalent in modern biology of the biblical notion of the divine spirit as the origin of life that transcends the limits of the organism? While historicity indicates the general character of reality in the perspective of biblical faith, the divine spirit, at once immanent in creation and transcending the creature, constitutes its living reality in its relation to an ecstatic beyond of self-giving and satisfaction. Since this includes the hope for resurrection and eternal life, the fourth question refers to the relation between time and eternity: Is there any positive relation conceivable of the concept of eternity to the spatiotemporal structure of the physical universe? This is one of the most neglected but also one of the most important questions in the dialogue between theology and science. It is unavoidable if the reality of God is to be related in a positive way to the mathematical structure of the spatiotemporal world of nature.

It will prove indispensable also in approaching the fifth and perhaps the most difficult question in the dialogue between theology and modern science, the question of eschatology: Is the Christian affirmation of an imminent end of this world that in some way invades the present somehow reconcilable with scientific extrapolations of the continuing existence of the universe for at least several billions of years ahead? Just to ask this question in a way that does not simply reduce biblical language to metaphor or dismiss it as mythological is extremely difficult. But this difficulty already arises with the third question regarding the spirit. And from the beginning of such a discourse it lurks behind the very term "God." It is only by exploring the function of "spirit"—involving a redefinition of that term, a clarification of the interrelation between time and eternity, and the issue of eschatology—that the term "God" in its biblical concreteness can be understood in its importance to the world of nature. The first two questions simply provide a starting point for such an exploration, one that will not allow theologians and scientists to talk on so different and unrelated levels as to reduce any agreement in terminology to mere equivocations.

Inertia and Divine Conservation

Is it conceivable, in view of the importance of contingency in natural processes, to revise the principle of inertia or at least its interpretation? The crucial importance of this question in the dialogue between science and theology is generally underestimated. Perhaps this is so because under the impact of deism the relation between God and the world was reduced to the origin of the world and especially of our planetary system. But as early as the fourteenth century the question of the conservation of finite reality had become more prominent in the discussion of the indispensability of a first cause regarding the interpretation of nature. William of Ockham rejected the view of the thirteenth century that in the order of existence the assumption of a first cause was necessary. He argued that in the sequence of generations it was quite natural that the later generation was alive while the former generations were already dead.

In order for a new generation to rise, the continuing existence of a first forebear is not required. In the same way there is no first cause; nor is its continuing existence required in order to account for the continuous rise of new beings in the world. If it were, the chain of natural causes could be traced back ad infinitum. But the need for preservation of what came into existence led Ockham to a different conclusion. If continued existence was not self-explanatory but required the continued activity of the cause that gave origin to the creature, then without the continued existence and activity of a first cause all its effects would vanish, whatever the mediation of their origin might be. Therefore, in Ockham's view, God was still indispensable in the explanation of the physical world because without God no finite reality could persist.

This was changed, however, when in the seventeenth century the principle of inertia was introduced in modern physics. It described an innate potential of persistence for any physical reality, whether in a state of rest or in a state of motion, unless it was disturbed by some other force. The far-reaching impact of this principle on the relation of physical reality to God went largely unnoticed. But the philosopher Hans Blumenberg, in an article published in 1970, demonstrated in some detail that the introduction of the principle of inertia in seventeenth-century physics was to replace the dependence of physical reality on God's activity of continuous creation with the idea of self-preservation, an idea that presumably was derived from Stoic traditions.[1]

Interestingly enough, René Descartes considered the principle of inertia still to be in need of some deeper foundation. He traced it back to the immutability of God in his dealings with his creation. Since Descartes still believed that everything created in each moment of its existence depended on the continuous activity of the creator, on his *creatio continua*, only the immutability of the creator could account for the stability in the order of creation, the basic manifestation of which is to be found in the tendency of everything to persevere in the status once acquired unless disturbed by other forces.[2] Later, Isaac Newton was content to use the principle of inertia in his *Principia naturae* (1687) without explicit reference to God (definitions 3 and 4). But Baruch Spinoza was the first to identify the essence of things with their perseverance in being, and thus he provided a metaphysical foundation for the emancipation of nature from its dependence on divine conservation, on a continuous concursus of a transcendent God.[3]

The emancipation from the creator God entailed in the principle of inertia did not apply only to individual natural bodies and beings which at the same time continued to undergo influences from outside themselves. Even more serious was the consequence that the system of the natural universe had to be conceived now as an interplay between finite bodies and forces without further need for recourse to God. When, almost one hundred years after Spinoza, Immanuel Kant again used the contingency of all finite reality as a starting point for developing his idea of God, he found himself confined to the puzzlement such contingency presented to human reason; he no longer could claim a direct dependence of contingent reality on God for its preservation.[4] On the other side, Christian apologetics, having accepted the new basis of natural philosophy provided by the principle of inertia, was now left to the unfortunate strategy of looking for gaps in the continuity of natural processes if it wanted to preserve certain occasions for divine interference in the natural world.

But perhaps the principle of inertia or of self-persistence is in fact not as self-evident as believed. If the stuff of the universe is finally made up of events rather than of solid bodies and if the latter are already the products of the regularities of events, then their inertia or self-persistence is no more self-evident than any other natural regularity. The "atomic" view of time and the awareness of the contingency of temporal sequence that kept Descartes from taking inertia as a self-evident principle and led him to seek its basis in the invariable faithfulness of the creator may be, after all, closer to the views of modern science than Spinoza's opposite view. Perhaps after three centuries the conclusion from physical phenomena to an action of God does no longer go so smoothly as at the time of Descartes. But if it depends on a combination of contingent conditions, the phenomenon of inertia may tacitly imply the framework of a field of force to provide the conditions for such a phenomenon to exist.[5]

Contingency, Irreversibility, and History

The second question squarely faces the issue of contingency and regularities of nature in its general form: *Is the reality of nature to be understood as contingent, and are natural processes to be understood as irreversible?* The combination of the two parts of the question suggests that irreversibility is related to contingency and may be rooted in it. In order to explain this, a number of steps are necessary before the impact of the issue on a theological view of the historicity of nature can become apparent.

First, contingent conditions, initial conditions as well as boundary conditions, are required for any formula of natural law to be applied. They are contingent at least in that they cannot be derived from the particular formula of law under consideration.

Second, the regularity itself, which is described by a formula of natural law, can be considered as contingent because its pattern represents a repeatable sequence of events, a sequence that, being temporal, must take place a first time before it is repeated and becomes a regular sequence.[6] The mathematical formula of a natural law may be valid without regard to time. The physical regularity that is described by such a formula is not independent of time and temporal sequence. But it is only that physical regularity which makes the mathematical formula a law of nature. This suggests that laws of nature are not eternal or atemporal because the fields of their application, the regularities of natural process, originate in the course of time. Thus it also becomes understandable that new patterns of regularity emerging in the sequence of time constitute a field of application for a new set of natural laws such that "the laws governing matter in a higher level of organization can never be entirely deduced from the properties of the lower levels."[7]

Third, if this consideration applies to all natural regularities in temporal sequences, it leads to a general thesis on irreversibility in natural processes. This irreversibility, which is based ultimately on the irreversibility of time, does not preclude the emergence of repeatable patterns of temporal sequence; but such an emergence itself becomes a contingent event. The regularity by itself therefore is only an abstraction—from the contingent process and context of its emergence. Therefore its explanatory potential is necessarily limited.

The irreversibility in natural processes is often argued for on different grounds, especially in relation to the law of entropy. This also has been applied to cosmology and has contributed to relativistic models of the universe such as the big bang theory. But the ultimate basis of irreversibility may rather be looked for, as Carl F. von Weizsäcker suggests, in the irreversibility of time.[8] Here, then, contingency and irreversibility may have their common root.

The theological interest in such considerations is due to the biblical understanding of reality as historical. It is intimately related to the biblical understanding of God the creator who acts freely and unrestrictedly not only in laying the foundations of the universe but also in the subsequent course of events. This "continuous creation" is basically characterized by contingency because future acts of God cannot be deduced from past course of events. Yet there emerge regularities and persistent forms of created reality giving expression to the faithfulness and identity of God in affirming the world that God created. The continuity of this creation can be characterized as the continuity of a history of God being engaged in with his creation. This historical continuity adds to the continuity that is expressed in the regularities of natural processes: while the description of those regularities in the form of "natural laws" abstracts from the contingent conditions of their occurrence, historical continuity comprises the contingency of events together with the emergence of regularities. Thus the category of history provides a more comprehensive description of the continuous process of nature. On the other hand, the continuity of that history in its biblical conception seems to be placed outside the created process, that is, within God himself. Thus we have to see whether this continuity also manifests itself inside the process of nature. This leads to the third question, which is concerned with the spirit of God.

Bible and Biology on the Origin of Life

Is there any equivalent in modern biology of the biblical notion of the divine spirit as the origin of life that transcends the limits of the organism? The question is focused on the phenomenon of life because in biblical writings the work of the spirit relates specifically to life. But it also relates to the created world in its entirety, as the initial words in the book of Genesis indicate.

In biblical traditions, life is not considered as a function of the organism. This constitutes a basic difference from the view of modern biology.[9] The life-giving power is seen as an agent that influences the organism from the outside. When it is called "spirit," one must not think of consciousness and intelligence in the first place. The spirit is, rather, a mysterious reality, comparable to the wind (John 3:8). When God breathes it into the creature which he built earlier, it comes alive (Gen. 2:7). Thus the person has a life in himself or herself, but only a limited share of it. In the event of death, "the dust returns to the earth as it was, and the spirit returns to God who gave it" (Eccl. 12:7). Further, this view of life as originating from a transcendent source is an indispensable presupposition for the hope in a resurrection to a new life beyond death. Only if the source of life transcends the organism is it conceivable that the individual be given a new life that is no longer separate from the divine spirit, the source of life, but permanently united with it as a "spiritual body" (1 Cor. 15:42–44).

These biblical conceptions quite obviously belong to a universe of discourse different from what modern biology has to tell about life and its origin. But they cannot easily be dismissed as transient with the culture of their time, because they possess far-reaching importance for basic affirmations of the Christian faith. If they are to be taken as carrying an important truth, however, it must be somehow present, if only in oblique form, in modern biological descriptions of life too.

Now, the living organism, in the view of modern biology, is not a closed system. It transcends itself by inhabiting a territory within an appropriate environment, and it literally lives "on" that environment. In its drives it relates to a future that transforms its own status of life. Sexuality is a particularly powerful manifestation of the ecstatic nature of life.

If one tries to develop a synthetic account of these phenomena, one may be led in a direction similar to that of Michael Polanyi's explanation of individual morphogenesis on the assumption of a "morphogenic field" that comprises all the boundary conditions of individual development.[10] Polanyi himself does not shy away from expanding this notion in conceiving the idea of a phylogenetic field that governs the process of evolution and that provides a perspective in which individual organisms are to be considered as singularizations; he says that "the evidence provided by the various branches of biology (including psychology)" seems "to cry out for the acknowledgement of a field as the agent of biotic performances."[11] At this point Polanyi's thought meets with Pierre Teilhard de Chardin's vision of point Omega at work in the process of evolution as the power of the divine spirit, although Teilhard does not use the field concept in describing the efficacy of that power in the same way as Polanyi.[12]

To the theologian the description of the evolution of life in terms of a generalized field theory must be extremely suggestive, because it seems to offer a modern language that possibly can express the biblical idea of the divine spirit as the power of life that transcends the living organism and at the same time is intimately present in the individual. In the perspective of such a field theory of life one may follow Polanyi's "logic of achievement" in the sequence of emergent forms of life and in his final vision of a "cosmic field which called forth all these centres by offering them a short-lived, limited, hazardous opportunity for making some progress of their own towards an unthinkable consummation."[13] But it is not by chance that Polanyi calls that consummation "unthinkable," because neither the eschatological presence of God's kingdom nor the Christian hope for the new life of a resurrection of the dead is imaginable as just another stage in the temporal sequence of the evolutionary process. It adds another dimension, the transfiguration of the temporal by the presence of the eternal.

Eternity and Space-Time

Is there any positive relation conceivable of the concept of eternity to the spatiotemporal structure of the physical universe? As I said, this is one of the most arduous but also one of the most important questions in the dialogue between theology and natural science. If eternity means the divine mode of being, then it is directly concerned with the question of how the reality of God is related to the spatiotemporal universe. Without an answer to the question regarding time and eternity the relation of God to this world remains inconceivable.

Eternity has been interpreted traditionally as timelessness, and in this interpretation its relation to time appears to be purely negative. But this contradicts the Christian hope for resurrection because that hope does not aim at a completely different life replacing the present one. Rather, it aims at a transformation of this present life to let it participate in the divine glory. Salvation cannot mean pure negation and annihilation of this present life, of this creation of God. Therefore in a Christian perspective time and eternity must have some positive relation. This is also implied in the doctrine of the incarnation, since that means a togetherness of the human and the divine in the person and life of Jesus Christ.

The notion of eternity certainly means unlimited presence. But this need not exclude the temporal that comes into existence once and passes again into nonexistence. The positive relation of the temporal to the eternal could mean that in the perspective of the eternal the temporal does not pass away, although in relation to other spatiotemporal entities it does. On the basis of this it is also conceivable that the lasting presence of the temporal before the eternal God may become the experience of the temporal itself, so that it experiences itself as it stands in the presence of God, vanishing in its contradiction to God or transformed in participation in his glory.

Such an inclusive interpretation of eternity in relation to temporal reality, however, requires a systematic way of relating the extensions of time and space to a conceptual model of eternity. Such a model should be mathematical in character in order to comprise the mathematical structures of space and time. A German mathematician, Günter Ewald of the University of Bochum, is developing such a model.[14] It is based on the notion of a field, just as the theory of relativity conceives of the spatiotemporal universe as a single field. According to Ewald, this notion can be expanded to include complex numbers beyond real numbers. Since in the level of complex numbers no linear sequence occurs, the transition from complex numbers to real numbers can be interpreted as a transition into spatiotemporal existence. Generally the field of complex numbers in its relation to real numbers can provide a model of the relation of eternity to spatiotemporal events.

It remains to be seen how far the explanatory power of this model goes. Does it explain not only the transition from the eternal to the temporal existence but also the manifestation of the eternal within the temporal sequence? According to Christian doctrine, such a manifestation of the eternal within temporal reality will occur in its fullness in the eschaton (last times), but by anticipation it occurred in the midst of the ongoing sequence of events in the resurrection of Jesus. This event persuaded the Christian community that the eternal Logos was incarnate in Jesus. The entire problem of miracles is related to the question of the anticipatory presence of the eschatological consummation. But there are also other and more ordinary modes of an anticipatory presence of the eternal in time. According to the Christian doctrine that the divine Logos had an important part even in the creation of the world, the logical structure that became manifest in the person and history of Jesus Christ should somehow be present in every creature. Just as Jesus' identity as the son of God is to be finally confirmed in his eschatological parousia, the essence of all things is realized presently only by anticipation and will be revealed finally in the ultimate future where the temporal will be reconstituted in the presence of the eternal. This is but one aspect of how every creature bears the imprint of the Logos. There also seems to be a tendency toward increasing participation in the divine spirit and Logos in the course of the evolution of creatures, approximating the eschatological presence of the eternal in the temporal. The human mind is distinguished by a unique degree of openness to the presence of the eternal which is expressed in the experience of an amplified presence that overlaps, though in a limited way, past and future events. The participation of the human mind in the eternal Logos through the ecstatic power of the spirit may account also for the possibility and specific character of human knowledge of the created world.

In a trinitarian perspective the work of the Logos and that of the spirit in the creation of the world belong closely together. Can this be expressed in a language that takes account of modern science? If von Weizsäcker's suggestion is followed, namely, that the ancient philosophical Logos doctrine can be reformulated in terms of modern information theory, then it does not seem completely inconceivable that a field theory of information can do justice to the cooperation of Logos and spirit in the creation of the world.[15]

Christian Eschatology and the Scientific "Universe"

The last question, that of eschatology, was already touched upon in connection with the work of the spirit and with the transfiguring presence of the eternal in the temporal. But it needs to be raised in its own right because it points to one of the most obvious conflicts between a worldview based on modern science and the Christian faith: *Is the Christian affirmation of an imminent end of this world that in some way invades the present somehow reconcilable with scientific extrapolations of the continuing existence of the universe for at least several billions of years ahead?*

To this question there are no easy solutions. Scientific predictions that in some comfortably distant future the conditions for life will no longer continue on our planet are hardly comparable to biblical eschatology. On the other hand, some people are always quick to expurgate the religious traditions from elements that seem to make no sense to one period in the development of scientific insight. Perhaps one should, rather, accept a conflict in such an important issue, accept it as a challenge to the human mind to penetrate deeper still into the complexities of human experience and awareness. It does not seem unreasonable to expect that a detailed exploration of the issues involved in the question concerning time and eternity may lead one day to more satisfactory ways including biblical eschatology in an interpretation of the natural world that should take appropriate account of modern science.

Notes

1. Hans Blumenberg, "Selbsterhaltung und Beharrung: Zur Konstitution der neuzeitlichen Rationalität," *Abhandlungen der Mainzer Akademie der Wissenschaften und der Literatur, geistes- und sozialwissenschaftliche Klasse*, jg. 1969, no. 11 (1970): 333–83; reprinted in *Subjektivität und Selbsterhaltung: Beiträge zur Diagnose der Moderne*, ed. Hans Ebeling (Frankfurt: Suhrkamp Verlag, 1976), 144–207.
2. Blumenberg, in Ebeling, *Subjektivität*, 182–85; and René Descartes, *Principia philosophiae* 2.36–37.
3. Blumenberg, in Ebeling, *Subjektivität*, 185–88.
4. Immanuel Kant, *Der einzig mögliche Beweisgrund für eine Demonstration des Daseins Gottes* (1763); cf. H. G. Redmann's commentary, *Gott und Welt: Die Schöpfungstheologie der vorkritischen Periode Kants* (Göttingen: Vandenhoeck & Ruprecht, 1962), 142–48, 98–99.
5. C. F. von Weizsäcker, in *Die Einheit der Natur* (Munich: Carl Hanser Verlag, 1971), 364, calls the principle of inertia "eine Folge der Wirkung des Universums auf das einzelne Urobjekt." This corresponds to the view of Albert Einstein (in his preface to Max Jammer, *Concepts of Space* [Cambridge: Harvard University Press, 1954]) that Isaac Newton introduced his concept of absolute space "als selbständige Ursache des Trägheitsverhaltens der Körper" in order to secure "dem klassischen Trägheitsprinzip (und damit dem klassischen Bewegungsgesetz) einen exakten Sinn." According to Einstein, the concept of absolute space (or its amplification to that of an "inertial system" including time could be overcome only when "der Begriff des körperlichen Objektes als Fundamentalbegriff der Physik allmählich durch den des Feldes ersetzt wurde," since then "die Einführung eines *selbständigen* Raumes" was no longer necessary. Einstein concluded: "Eine andere Möglichkeit für die Überwindung des Intertialsystems als den über die Feldtheorie hat bis jetzt niemand gefunden."
6. See chapter 4, "Contingency and Natural Law," esp. 105–10.
7. A. R. Peacocke, *Science and the Christian Experiment* (London: Oxford University Press, 1971), 87.
8. Von Weizsäcker, *Die Einheit*, 239–40.
9. More detail on this argument is given in chapter 5, "The Doctrine of the Spirit and the Task of a Theology of Nature."

10. Michael Polanyi, *Personal Knowledge: Towards a Post-Critical Philosophy*, 2d ed. (New York: Harper & Row, 1962), 356.
11. Ibid., 402. For the generalized field concept, see 398–400.
12. See my discussion of Pierre Teilhard de Chardin's views on energy in chapter 6, "Spirit and Energy."
13. Polanyi, *Personal Knowledge*, 405. Polanyi's use of the field concept should not be mistaken as just another form of vitalism. It is, rather, opposed to the vitalist assumption, such as Aristotelian entelechy, of a finalistic principle working within the organism. Contrary to this, the field concept involves no finality; nor does it dwell in the organism as some occult quality distinct from its more ordinary aspects open to physical description. The field concept, rather, offers an integrative framework for a comprehensive description of all aspects of organic life, including its interaction with its ecological context.
14. See Günter Ewald, "Bemerkungen zum Begriff von Raum und Zeit in der Physik," in *Gott-Geist-Materie: Theologie und Naturwissenschaft im Gespräch*, ed. H. Dietzfelbinger and L. Mohaupt (Hamburg: Lutherisches Verlagshaus, 1980), 79–86.
15. Von Weizsäcker, *Die Einheit*, 342–66.

2

The Doctrine of Creation
and Modern Science

From the eighteenth century to the beginning of the twentieth century the relations between science and theology were marked by an increasing mutual alienation. In the course of this century, however, there has emerged a series of efforts to bridge the gulf that had developed. In England these efforts started as early as the second half of the last century, when there was an attempt to make a theologically positive evaluation of the theory of evolution in order to integrate it into a Christian vision of the world and of salvation history. A considerable number of scientists, especially biologists, took part in these efforts, particularly in Britain and in America. Germany did not really participate in these efforts, although in the beginning of this century the remarkable Erlangen theologian Karl Beth did develop a similar approach in apologetics. Unfortunately, Beth has been largely forgotten. In Germany, the initiative to dialogue came from a number of leading physicists, beginning with Max Planck, but it did not take actual shape until the early postwar period. The dialogue was more difficult here because the concept of evolution was not used as a common denominator for both scientific and theological views.

Even to this day the history of the alienation between the natural sciences and theology has not been cleared up. Everywhere the systematic discussions of those substantial issues which resulted in the process of mutual alienation and which continued to be effective until the present day have rarely gotten off the ground. Part of the explanation of this failure may be that not until the last decades has the discipline of the history of science provided results that make it possible to deal with these problems on the basis of sufficient information and a methodical procedure. I think here especially of the contributions of Max Jammer and Alexandre Koyré, of Mary Hesse and William Berkson as helpful examples.

Inertia as a Theological Problem

The reasons for the history of alienation between science and theology have to be looked for on both sides. In the beginning there was the fatal lack of appreciation by theology and church, not only on the Catholic but also on the Protestant side, of the new doctrine of Copernicus. Both Martin Luther and Philip Melanchthon failed to realize the importance of Copernicus because of their reliance on the literal authority of the Bible. In one of his table talks in 1539 Luther said he would rather believe Holy Scripture that reports in the book of Joshua (10:12–13) that Joshua ordered the sun to stand still and not the earth.[1] This type of biblical fundamentalism and the resulting suspicion against the new astronomy continued in German Lutheran theology until the early eighteenth century. In the period of the Enlightenment, theologians tried to adapt the biblical seven-day scheme of creation to the new scientific picture of the natural world. But in the meantime other and even more fundamental problems had surfaced.

These problems emerged from drawing the consequences of the new mechanical physics for understanding the basic relationship between God and world. Of special importance was the introduction of the principle of inertia. Already in the thought of Descartes this principle led to an emancipation of the natural processes from their dependence on God, although the general framework of Descartes's ideas on the creation of the world and on its need for continuous preservation by God was still quite traditional. Descartes's formulation of the principle of inertia stated that each part of natural matter tends to preserve its status as long as this is not changed by external factors. Such changes, however, can be initiated only by other parts of natural matter, that is, by other bodies. The reason for this assumption was Descartes's concept of God. On the one hand, he still considered it necessary to give a reason for the principle of inertia itself. Descartes did not yet take inertia simply as manifestation of a *vis insita*, a force of perseverance within the body itself, as Newton did later. Rather, Descartes took it to manifest the immutability of God, who—as far as he is concerned—

preserves his creature in the same form in which he created it. The same principle of divine immutability, on the other hand, prevented Descartes from ascribing to God the changes that occur in the world of creation. All changes, therefore, had to be interpreted as resulting from the actions of other bodies, the presupposition of this being that bodies always are in some form of movement which they transfer upon one another by pressure and push. When the assumption that movement is intrinsic to the bodies themselves was combined with the principle of inertia, the need for the cooperation of God as first cause became superfluous in the explanation of natural processes.

Baruch Spinoza explicitly drew that consequence of the mechanical explanation of nature, and he protected it against theological suspicion by the argument that the independent functioning of the world's mechanism gives expression to the perfection of its divine author and of his work. In the early eighteenth century, Protestant theologians realized the danger, however, that in this way God would be separated from the creation. Johann Franz Buddeus argued that in the final analysis this amounts to a denial of God's very existence, because God becomes superfluous.

It was the same reason that induced Isaac Newton to reject Descartes's reduction of movement to the concept of body and to replace it by his conception of force as *vis impressa*, as a force that may impress movements upon bodies even over great distances in space. But at this point, with his general conception of force, Newton was not successful, at least not in the judgment of his own age. Instead, the combination of Newton's interpretation of inertia in terms of a force that is inherent in bodies with the reduction of force to a body and to its mass contributed in a decisive way in the course of the eighteenth century to the removal of God from the explanation of nature.

The Concept of God as an Explanation of Nature?

Protestant theology since the early nineteenth century, in Germany at least, developed an attitude of resignation over against this development. In order to explain this fact, it is important to see that there were also theological reasons at work. The rapid development of historical-critical investigation of the biblical writings had dissolved the traditional understanding of the authority of the Bible based on the divine inspiration of its wording. The biblical authors' conceptions of the order of nature came now to be interpreted as an expression of a primitive understanding of the natural order, as an expression of some archaic, "mythical" conception of the world, or even the perspective of cultic life, as found in the biblical seven-day scheme of creation. Therefore, as early as 1814 even a rather traditional theologian like Karl Gottlieb Bretschneider considered it "a lost effort to try a physical demonstration of the words of creation as reported by Moses."[2]

After that time, theological apologetics increasingly abstained from theological interpretation or criticism of the foundations of natural science and embarked on the unhappy strategy of looking for the gaps in the scientific explanation of nature. It was largely because of this strategy that Darwin's theory of evolution could be perceived and rejected as a fundamental challenge of faith in God. When the theory of evolution had come to prevail in the scientific world, many theologians in Germany withdrew to a position claiming an incomparability of the theological and the scientific descriptions of the world. This was quite contrary to the situation in England and in America, where an early breakthrough to a positive interpretation of natural evolution took place. The most remarkable example of the theological retreat from a discussion of the scientific description of nature was Karl Barth, who in the preface of his doctrine of creation in his *Church Dogmatics*[3] decided that in principle a theological doctrine of creation should not concern itself with scientific descriptions and results.

One may point to the work of Karl Heim as an example of a different attitude in German theology. Yet even Heim, for all his competence in conversations with scientists, was more concerned to relativize the level of scientific conceptualizing and description of nature in toto by presenting it as a form of thought, over against which theology represents a quite different form of thought. The two forms of thought are not "polarized" but, as Heim said, "superpolar." Therefore, even Heim did not really enter into a theological appropriation and critique of the conceptual foundations of natural science. In order to do so he would have needed a clear perception of the interrelations between the history of philosophy and the history of the formation of scientific conceptuality; and in this area he did not employ the necessary information. In positive contrast to Barth, nevertheless, Heim was aware that theological talk about God as creator (and therefore any talk about God) remains empty, if it is not relatable to the scientific description of nature.

In the modern world, scientific theories have achieved such a high degree of common recognition of validity that in public consciousness the primary, if not exclusive, competence for valid assertions about the reality of the world is attributed to the sciences. It is impossible to change this fact by mere decree. If theologians want to conceive of God as the creator of the real world, they cannot possibly bypass the scientific description of that world. Certainly, theological assertions concerning the world are not formulated on the same level with scientific hypotheses of natural law. Nevertheless, they have to be related to scientific reasoning. Whether this is possible or not must be discussed on the level of philosophical (or maybe theological) reflection on the assertions of the natural sciences. Of course it is possible to suspect that such a reflection may remain something secondary and arbitrary in comparison to the scientific statements themselves. It may be considered a form of thought that remains irrelevant on the level of the demonstration and validity of scientific hypotheses and theories. Positivistic philosophy of science used to describe the situation in such a way.

Now research in the history of science has suggested a different perspective. In contrast to other positivists, Karl Popper even in his earlier period admitted that metaphysical convictions of innovative scientists may belong to the subjective factors conditioning the formation of their scientific hypotheses and theories. Yet his former student William Berkson uses the history of field physics to show that certain metaphysical conceptions not only have individual importance but also accompany or even guide the development of entire branches of natural science. If this is so, the philosophical origin of scientific conceptuality can no longer be regarded as something external and irrelevant as far as the scientific theories themselves are concerned. Certainly, the demonstration of the scientific usefulness of such conceptualities and of their use in scientific formulas has to operate on a different level; but even so, they remain dependent on the broader philosophical intuition from which they were derived. The interrelation of scientific and philosophical conceptuality determines the framework for a rational discussion of the question whether theological assertions about the *world as creation* are relatable to the scientific description of the natural world.

The rest of this chapter intends to suggest how the subject matter of the theological doctrine of creation implies that it is impossible to appropriate the scientific description of the world of nature in the way just indicated. It is not my intention, however, to discuss the claims of an alternative "creationist" science. I do not think that the creationists are really in a position to challenge the established theories of modern science. Theology has to relate to the science that presently exists rather than invent a different form of science for its own use.

Creation and Contingency

The traditional doctrine of creation distinguishes between creation as an act of God and creatures as the products of divine activity. In dealing with creation as an act of God the correspondence between creation, conservation, and the divine government of the world has been discussed along with questions such as the meaning of the participation of Christ or the divine Logos and of the Holy Spirit in the work of creation. The theological treatment of the different creatures is traditionally concerned with the order of creation in the sequence of the divine production following more or less the biblical presentation of the work of creation taking place in a sequence of seven days. The attribution of certain creatures to a certain "day" of creation has been the dominant form in theological tradition of conceiving of an order of nature.

Obviously there are connections—not only correspondences but also differences—between the traditional theological account of the formation of the world and the scientific description of nature, especially with reference to the description of the different creatures and the sequence of their appearance or emergence. There are also such connections already with the theological doctrines of creation, conservation, and government of the world, and these raise fundamental questions regarding our understanding of the world. Therefore the following considerations focus primarily on these issues.

In the first place, the theological affirmation that the world of nature proceeds from an act of divine creation implies the claim that the existence of the world as a whole and of all its parts is contingent. The existence of the whole world is contingent in the sense that it need not be at all. It owes its existence to the free activity of divine creation. So does every single part of the world. In the second place, there is a close tie between this contingency and the structure of time insofar as the possibility of existence is tied to the future. The structural modes of reality are rooted in temporality.

Affirmations about the contingency of the world at large and of all its parts already imply a close connection between creation and conservation. The world was not simply put into existence once, at the beginning of all things, in such a way that it would have been left to its own afterward. Rather, every creature is in need of conservation of its existence in every moment; and such conservation is, according to theological tradition, nothing else but a continuous creation. This means that the act of creation did not take place only in the beginning. It occurs at every moment. Accordingly, in the traditional theological doctrine of creation the activity of every creature is dependent on divine cooperation, a *concursus divinus*. There is no activity and no product of creative activity in the world without divine cooperation.

The divine activity operates without detriment to the contingency and immediacy of singular actions, which has been identified in the theological tradition with the idea of divine governance of the world. It is due to this divine government of creation that the sequence of contingent events and created forms takes the shape of a continuous process toward the divine goal of an ultimate completion and glorification of all creation.

The three aspects of conservation, concurrence, and government have been often taken together into the concept of divine providence. The difference, however, between the act of creation in the beginning and the activity of divine providence in the course of an already existing world, as well as further subdistinctions of the concept of providence itself, must not obscure the unity of divine action in all these respects.

This entire conception of God's creative activity was deeply challenged in the seventeenth century because of the introduction of the principle of inertia. The German philosopher Hans Blumenberg[4] has repeatedly put his finger on this remarkable event, an event of far-reaching importance in the history of modern times. The principle of inertia as formulated by Descartes means that no longer is the continuous existence of any given state of affairs in need of explanation but only the occurrence of any changes of this status. This principle does not yet abolish the notion of a creation in the beginning, but a continuous conservation of what once was created becomes unnecessary. This consequence seems to be inevitable, if inertia in contrast to Descartes is understood as a force of self-preservation inherent in the body, a *vis insita*. On this basis, a transcendent conservation (*Fremderhaltung*) of nature becomes indeed superfluous. In a similar way the mechanical interpretation of the changes occurring to the bodies in terms of a transfer of movement renders the assumption of a divine cooperation in the activities of the creatures superfluous. Thus deism must be seen as the consequence of the introduction of the principle of inertia in modern physics.

In view of the historical importance of this development, any contemporary discussion between theology and science should focus in the first place on the question of what modern science, and especially modern physics, can say about the contingency of the universe as a whole and of every part in it. This is, of course, a more general formulation of the basic issue inherent in the affirmations of the dependence of the natural world on its creation and conservation by God.

A discussion of this question of contingency in natural science took place at the Protestant Academy of Research at Heidelberg during the 1960s. The subject was treated by way of reflection on the character, range, and limits of scientific language and especially on the correlation of law and contingency. There was a resulting agreement to the effect that each scientific hypothesis of law describes uniformities in the behavior of the object of such affirmations. The object itself, however, is contingently given in relation to its hypothetical description as a case where the affirmed law obtains. This element of contingency in the givenness of the object, however, is usually not explicitly focused upon in scientific statements. The focus is rather on the uniformities that can be expressed in equations. It is accepted as fact that those uniformities occur in a substratum that is not exhausted by them.

On reflection, however, the applicability of scientific formulas to concrete cases of natural processes requires initial and marginal conditions that are contingent in relation to the uniformity affirmed in the equation as such. Also, the natural constants that become part of the equation are considered contingent factors. This means that the description of nature by hypothetical statements of natural law presupposes their material as contingently given. The scientific formulas do not focus on this contingency, therefore, because their intention is to formulate uniformities that occur in the natural phenomena, their contingency notwithstanding. This focusing on the aspect of law constitutes the specifically abstract character of a scientific description of natural processes.

If this consideration is correct, it yields far-reaching consequences: the scientific affirmations of law cannot be considered as complete and exhaustive descriptions of the natural processes. They are only approximations, although they may be more than sufficiently precise for most practical purposes. The connection between events admits, however, another form of description which does not focus on uniformities in abstraction from the unique and contingent sequence of singular events. Rather, it describes the kind of connection that is to be constituted in the course of the contingent sequence itself and that can be perceived, therefore, only at the end of the sequence in question. In the perspective of such a description, the sequence of events is not considered as exchangeable cases, where a common formula of law applies according to the scheme: "if A, then B." Rather, the sequence is here perceived as a historical sequence, as a unique and irreversible process.

The two descriptions do not necessarily relate to different kinds of processes. The same process admits the description of cases of general laws as well as the description of individual, historical sequences. The description of a sequence of events as a historical process may be less abstract than its scientific description; but it presupposes more information about the individual sequence and its phases, while the description of the same sequence as a case of general law presupposes a knowledge of other comparable processes.

In theological discourse—in distinction from scientific descriptions, with the possible exception of the discipline of natural history—the sequence of events is taken as a historical sequence. The preference of theology for historical presentation of reality is related to its interest in nature's contingency. This does not necessarily mean that theology should treat everything in a "narrative" form. Rather, much analytic and constructive reflection is necessary before the theologian can hope to tell the story of God's creation with any degree of plausibility. Even historical narration presupposes a prior reconstruction of the process the historian reports.

The particularity of theology in looking at the world as history also applies to the uniformities that occur in the course of natural processes and to the enduring forms of natural reality that emerge on the basis of such uniformities. In the theological perspective such uniformities, a substratum of the hypothesis of natural law, as well as the enduring forms of natural reality are considered as contingent in the same way as any single event. The laws of nature appear to the theologian as contingent products of the creative freedom of God. The unity of contingency and continuity in the creative activity of God as well as in its products is rooted, according to a theological interpretation of the world, in God's faithfulness. Although God's action is contingent and underivable in each singular moment, still it keeps a connection to what happened before, while the future form of manifestation of God's faithfulness remains unforeseeable.

Field and Spirit

The reflections on the interrelation of contingency and natural law provide only a very abstract and formal framework for the interpretation of scientific and theological statements about the world of nature. These considerations do not yet relate to the specific object of natural science. If one remembers the history of modern science, it is obvious that its theories have been related in the first place to the task of describing the movements and changes in natural phenomena. For this purpose modern physics developed the concepts of force and energy that act upon bodies and produce changes within them. By introducing the concept of force, Newton modified Descartes's interpretation of the changes in natural bodies as a result of movement. On the one hand, this modification broadened the concept of mass, so that the product of mass and acceleration now allows for the measurement of force; but on the other hand, and above all, the basic concept of force itself took the general form of *vis impressa*. In contrast to Descartes, Newton took into account the possibility of immaterial forces that act in a way analogous to the activity of the soul upon the body. He took gravitation as an example of such a form and considered it as an expression of the immaterial activity of God moving the universe by means of space (A. Koyré).[5] Apparently it was precisely these theological implications of Newton's conception of immaterial forces causing material changes that provoked the criticism of his idea of force through the eighteenth century and farther until the work of Mach and Hertz, as Max Jammer suggested.[6] The tendency on a certain line of the development of modern physics to reduce all forces to bodies or "masses" (Hertz) had antitheological implications: If all forces would proceed from bodies or masses, then the understanding of nature would be so thoroughly separated from the idea of God—who is not a body— that theological language about a divine activity in the processes of the natural world would become simply unintelligible and absurd.

After this has been said, the implicit theological relevance of the field theories of Michael Faraday and his successors becomes evident. The main point of the field concept was to turn around the relation between force and body. To Faraday, the body was but a manifestation of the force that he conceived as an independent reality prior to the body, and he did so in conceiving forces in terms of fields. His vision was to reduce all the different forces to a single field of force that determines all the changes in the natural universe. In 1974, William Berkson showed that this metaphysical vision formed the basis of Faraday's field physics and the point of departure for the different experiments he devised and for the relatively limited demonstrations of the reality of fields that he achieved by those experiments. The decisive point in Faraday's grand vision was to conceive of body and mass as secondary phenomena, a concentration of force at particular places and points of the field. The material particle appears as the point where the lines of force converge and form a "cluster" that persists for some time.[7]

The turn toward the field concept in the development of modern physics has theological significance. This is suggested not only by its opposition toward the tendency to reducing the concept of force to bodies or masses but also because field theories from Faraday to Einstein claim a priority for the whole over the parts. This is of theological significance, because God has to be conceived as the unifying ground of the whole universe if he is to be conceived as creator and redeemer of the world. The field concept could be used in theology to make the effective presence of God in every single phenomenon intelligible. But does not such a use of the field concept ask too much of a term of natural science? Would its use in theology amount to more than equivocal language which had little in common with the meaning of the word in physics? In addition, does not such language misuse the idea of God as if it referred to a factor in the explanation of the world, if not even to one physical force?

The answer to scrupulous questions such as these can refer to the fact, in the first place, that the field concept was originally a metaphysical concept. The metaphysical idea of a field that inspired the modern field theories from Faraday to Einstein is traceable back to the pre-Socratics. It is to be found in Anaximenes who conceived of the air as cause and origin of all things, which supposedly had been built as concentrations of this thin element. It was Jammer who identified here the historical origin of all field theories, in the German dictionary of the history of philosophical terms.[8] In the Greek language, air was also named *pneuma*, and it is not by accident that in one of the fragments of Anaximenes *pneuma* and *aer* are used side by side.[9]

According to Jammer, the direct predecessor of the field concept in modern physics was the Stoic doctrine of the divine *pneuma*, which was conceived as a most subtle matter that penetrates everything and holds the cosmos together by the powerful tension between its different parts, that accounts for their cohesiveness as well as for the different movements and qualities of things. The Stoic doctrine of *pneuma* had an important impact on the patristic theology of the divine spirit and especially on its descriptions of the cosmological function of the spirit in creation. From the point of view of the early Christian fathers there was only one major difficulty connected with the Stoic conception of the *pneuma:* The Stoics conceived of it as a subtle material element. This was unacceptable to the Christian theologians, because they could not imagine God to be a material body. They opted, rather, for the Platonic conception of the divine reality as purely spiritual.

Difficulties of this sort no longer burden the field concept of modern physics, at least if no ether is considered necessary for the expansion of waves within the field. Thus the major theological difficulty with the Stoic field concept has been removed by its modern development; and since the field concept as such corresponds to the old concept of *pneuma* and was derived from it in the history of thought, theologians should consider it obvious to relate also the field concept of modern physics to the Christian doctrine of the dynamic presence of the divine spirit in all of creation. Such a way of using the field concept would certainly correspond to the connection that Christian patristics established between the biblical affirmations about the divine spirit as origin of all life and the Stoic doctrine of the *pneuma*.

In substance there is a much closer connection here than that with the Aristotelian doctrine of movement which gained such a fatal significance in medieval scholasticism and in early modern theology. It was the reduction of movement to bodies in Aristotelian physics that became a point of departure of the mechanical doctrine of movement in early modernity and consequently of the difficulties it created for theology. In contrast to the mechanical model of movement by push and pressure, the field concept could be celebrated as inauguration of a spiritual interpretation of nature.

This is particularly true in the case of Faraday's vision of reducing all material phenomena to a universal field of force.[10] However, the metaphysical intention of Albert Einstein took a different direction aiming at a reduction of the concept of force to a geometrical interpretation of gravitation that reduces the concept of force to a geometrical description of forceless movement of bodies in curved spaces.[11] In this connection one may remember Einstein's skeptical remark on the indeterminancy of quantum physics: "The old one doesn't play at dice." According to the presentation of Einstein's doctrine by Berkson, he was primarily interested in keeping the laws and properties of field invariant. Could it be that religious options were effective in the background of the conceptual differences between Faraday's concept of a field of force and Einstein's idea of the geometrical character of cosmic field? Could these be different interpretations of the Jewish idea of creation either in the line of the immutability of the law of the cosmos or in the line of God's powerful presence in the world?

To be sure, even a cosmic field conceived along the lines of Faraday's thought as a field of force would not be identified immediately with the dynamic activity of the divine spirit in creation. In every case the different models of science remain approximations in that they are all conceived under the point of view of natural law, of

uniform structures in natural processes. Therefore theological assertions of field structure of the divine spirit's activity in the cosmos
will remain different from field theories in physics. The difference
may be illustrated by two examples, one of them connected with the
question of how the different parts of the cosmic field are related to
the field itself and the other one dealing with the role of contingency
and time in the understanding of a cosmic field.

The first example carries the theologian into the territory of the
old dogmatic doctrine of angels. This fact alone could be sufficient
to distinguish the theological use of the field concept from that of
physics. Traditional theology conceived of angels as immaterial,
spiritual realities and powers who in distinction from the divine
spirit are nevertheless finite realities. Their activities were related
to the natural as well as to the historical world of human beings,
either as messengers of God or as acting in God's authority or by
way of demonic emancipation from God. From the point of view
of the field structure of spiritual dynamics one could consider
identifying the subject matter intended in the conception of angels
with the emergence of relatively independent parts of the cosmic
field. However, according to theological tradition, angels are personal spirits who decide for or against God. One need only recall
the fact that the concept of person in phenomenology of religion is
related to the impact of more or less incomprehensible "powers,"
the direction of which toward human beings and their world is
taken as evidence of a kind of "will," which, however, must not
suggest further anthropomorphic features. If one considers this
background of the biblical language about angels as personal realities, they may very well be related to fields of forces or dynamic
spheres, the activity of which may be experienced as good or bad.
Still, the difference of such a conception of angels from the later
doctrines of medieval scholastics as well as Protestant orthodoxy
would be obvious.

Space and Time

The other example concerning the relation of a theological use of
the field concept to time leads to even more complex problems. This
is so, because the field concept is closely related to space. Now there
are a number of good reasons—suggested by both philosophical and
scientific thought—to consider time and space as inseparable. Einstein's field concept comprises space, time, and energy. It takes the
form of a geometrical description, and this seems to amount to a

spatialization of time. The totality of space, time, and energy or force are all properties of a cosmic field.

Long before our own age a theological interpretation of this subject matter had been proposed, and it was Isaac Newton who offered this proposal. It too referred everything to space or, more precisely, to the correlation of space and force as in the case of a force like gravitation acting at a distance. Newton's well-known conception of space as sensory of God (*sensorium Dei*) did not intend to ascribe to God an organ of perception, the like of which God does not need, according to Newton, because of divine omnipresence. Rather, Newton took space as a medium of God's creative presence at the finite place of his creatures in creating them. The idea of Newton was easily mistaken as indicating some monstrously pantheistic conception of God similar to that found in Leibniz's polemics against Newton.

The basic argument of Newton or his spokesman Samuel Clarke was, however, widely discussed in the eighteenth century and has been taken up even in Kant's *Critique of Pure Reason*. In its first part, the transcendental aesthetics, the priority of infinite space over every conception of partial spaces was Kant's decisive argument for the intuitive character of space. The theological implications of this idea, however, were not even mentioned by Kant in this connection. More comprehensive consideration of the priority of the infinite over every finite experience had been affirmed already by Descartes's decisive argument in his thesis that the idea of God is the prior condition in the human mind for the possibility of any other idea, even that of the ego itself. If Kant had considered the full implications of the priority of the infinite over a finite conception, his phenomenalism would have become impossible, because the subject of experience itself belongs to those things which become conceivable only on the basis of the intuition of the infinite.

Samuel Alexander was quite correct to challenge Kant at this point in his book *Space, Time and Deity*.[12] Alexander himself, however, in distinction from Newton, conceived of infinite time and space in such a way as to attribute priority to time. The weakness of Newton's contribution to the subject matter is in the first place due to his deficient conception of time simply in terms of duration. Perhaps this deficiency is even responsible, at least in part, for Newton's poor appreciation of the doctrine of the Trinity. In any event, a trinitarian interpretation of the relation of God to the world is closely connected with time and history in the divine economy of salvation.

A discussion of the concept of time and of its importance in the field concept requires considerations that can be hardly touched upon in the context of the present reflections. But this much may be said: In Kant's transcendental aesthetics—in the case of time as well as in the case of space—the infinite has priority over any finite part. In the case of time, this brings Kant's argument into close contact with Plotinus's conception of time in distinction from the Aristotelian one. Plotinus argued that only on the basis of the perfect wholeness of life, an understanding of the nature of time is possible.[13] The whole of time, according to Plotinus, cannot be conceived as the whole of a sequence of moments, because the sequence of temporal moments can be indefinitely extended by adding further units. But according to Plotinus, time and the sequence of its units are understandable only under presupposition of the idea of a complete wholeness of life, which Plotinus conceived under the name of eternity (*aiōn*). In his conception the total unity of the whole of life is indispensable in the interpretation of the time sequence, because it hovers over that sequence as the future wholeness that is intended in every moment of time, so that the significance of eternity for the interpretation of time in Plotinus results in a primacy of the future concerning the nature of time. Not before Martin Heidegger's analysis of time was this insight rediscovered, and even here in only a limited way, limited to the experience of time in human existence.

The theological significance of the priority of eternity in the conception of time and of the consequent priority of the future is obvious, obvious at least in the contemporary context of theological discussion under the impact of the rediscovery of the meaning of eschatology in the message of Jesus and in early Christianity in general. When Augustine adapted Plotinian ideas about time, the situation was different. The primacy of the eschatological future in the understanding of time was not considered important; instead, Augustine focused upon the relation of the individual soul to time and eternity. His concentration on the subjective experience of time provided the direction for subsequent discussions of the subject all the way to Kant and Heidegger. Yet Augustine's psychological analysis of the experience of time presupposes the Plotinian ontology of time. This is particularly evident in Augustine's famous idea that the soul is the place of some continuous presence in the flow of momentary events. His account of this continuous presence in terms of a distension of the soul (*distentio animi*) stretching across the remembered past and the expected future conceives the duration of the soul as a form of participation in eternity.

This brings us back to the relation between theology and science in the understanding of time. If space is to be described as the form of simultaneity of phenomena, then the spatialization of time in physics—already in the preparation of a homogeneous time by the scientific techniques of time measurement and further then in the model of space-time or of a universal field comprising space, time, and energy—may be described as an extrapolation of all limited participation in the eternal presence of God, a participation that is granted to us in the experience of our duration in the flow of time. Spatialization, then, is not a mere fiction, as Henri Bergson suspected. Rather, it is rooted in the experience of "duration," the experience that was basic in Bergson's own thought but is also to be understood as constitutive of simultaneity in space as well as of continuity in the sequence of day and night, of summer and winter, all of which were early related to the movements of the skies. The cosmic clocks of the seemingly circular movements of the stars, especially of sun and moon, form the basis for our human division of time into equal segments. Nevertheless, no part of time is completely homogeneous in comparison to any other. This is already a consequence of the irreversibility of the time sequence. Therefore the spatialization of time in physics remains a mere approximation, even in the model of cosmic field, to the comprehensive unity of the process of the universe in the irreversible sequence of its history as seen from the perspective of divine eternity.

In distinction from the perspective of physics, the theologian looks at the universal field with the dimensions of space, time, and energy from the point of view of the eschatological future. Certainly, this theological perspective is in its own way limited to approximations. This is obvious in view of the inevitable lack in theological descriptions of the kind of precision available to science. This lack of precision is due to the fact that theology concerns itself with the contingent historicity of reality and with its contingent origin in the incomprehensible God who is incomprehensible precisely in his creative transcendence. Duns Scotus already recognized the limitation of theological knowledge in the fact that all theology knows God as well as other individual realities only through general concepts, while God's knowledge (if we are entitled to use that term in relation to God at all) grasps the variety of individual existence in one simultaneous act, in the form of an intuitive knowledge.

The Creatures of Creation

It seems appropriate to conclude this survey of problems connected with the doctrine of creation by turning at least briefly to the other side of that doctrine, to the products of the divine act of creation and to the emerging sequence of creatures.

The Priestly report on creation in the Bible presented the order of creation already as a sequence of creatures that are related to the sequence of days within the week of God's work. They rise one after another: first the light of day in distinction from the darkness at night, then water and the vault of heaven, then earth, vegetation, and the stars, followed by the animals of the sea and birds, until finally animals appear and populate the land, and at last the human being. In the perspective of contemporary information about the course of nature the sequence of forms would have to look different in certain particular cases. The Priestly report is, of course, colored by the natural science of its own day. A telling example of this is the conception of a separation of the waters by the massive building of the "vault of heaven." This vault separates the waters below from those above and provides the initial condition for a mechanical process, that is, that the waters below the vault, because their continuous supply from the upper ocean in heaven is cut off, recede to the deeper places, so that the solid ground shows up (Gen. 1:6, 9ff.). The same mechanism works the other way, when the "windows" that had been placed in the "vault of heaven" get opened (Gen. 7:11). The consequences are reported in the story of the flood.

The cosmology that comes to expression in this idea of a vault of heaven is very impressive but need not oblige the believer of the twentieth century. The theological doctrine of creation should take the biblical narrative as a model in that it uses the best available knowledge of nature in its own time in order to describe the creative activity of God (E. Schlink). This model would not be followed if theology simply stuck to a standard of information about the world that became obsolete long ago by further progress of experience and methodical knowledge.

The features that show in particular the historical relativity of some information in the Priestly reports include the relatively late creation of stars. That they appear as late as in the fourth day (Gen. 1:14ff.) and only in the utilitarian function of "lamps" is certainly due to the struggle of Israel's faith against those gods of the ancient Orient who were connected with sun or moon or other heavenly bodies. A certain degree of overreaction is also obvious at this point. In our present situation this is no longer an urgent problem of theology. Much more remarkable, however, than the necessary revisions in detail concerning the sequence of creative forms as reported in the first chapter of the Bible is the extent of substantial analogies between our contemporary and those ancient ideas about the origin and development of creation: the light in the beginning; human beings at the end of the sequence; the beginning of vegetation as a presupposition of animal life; the close kinship between human beings and mammals (the land animals) as creatures of one and the same, the sixth, day of creation. Above all, the scheme of a sequence of steps is still shared by the modern view. Certainly the sequence of steps appears from a modern perspective as an evolutionary process leading from primitive to more complex or higher organized forms. It is at this point that we identify the deepest difference between the biblical and the modern conception of a sequence of forms in the process of the creation.

The resistance of many theologians during the nineteenth and early twentieth centuries against the theory of evolution was largely caused by their apprehension that the doctrine of evolution would do away with all immediate dependence of the particular creatures on God's activity by deriving the higher forms from their predecessors. This discussion is no longer important at present, not only because the doctrine of evolution has been victorious in shaping the cultural consciousness but also because a further development of the doctrine of evolution itself went beyond that dispute. Presently, the proponents of an epigenetic interpretation of evolution in terms of an "emergent evolution" emphasize that later forms cannot be simply derived from earlier and lower ones. C. Lloyd Morgan's title *Emergent Evolution* of 1923 has almost become the catchword of a metaphysical concept of nature, because "emergence" means that on each level of evolution something new and underivable arises. Theodosius Dobzhansky could even call evolution "a source of novelty."[14]

In his *Ecumenical Dogmatics*, the Lutheran theologian Edmund Schlink identified the difference between the modern understanding of the sequence of natural forms and that of the Priestly report in the Bible to be rooted in the fact

> that, according to the biblical conception, the autonomous activity of the creatures is bound to the framework of their concrete order which was given to them in the beginning, while the picture emerging from modern research has been increasingly such that the concrete species of reality developed from the autonomous activity of the creatures before them.[15]

Even the Priestly report, however, knows and uses the idea that God's creative activity can be mediated through creatures. This is said especially with respect to the earth which, according to God's demand, produces the different forms of vegetation. This shows that there is no opposition in principle between the biblical conception of God's creative activity and the idea that this activity is mediated through creatures.

Something else, however, is missing completely in the biblical report, something that has become extremely important in the modern description of nature. This is the derivation of more complex forms from elementary processes, a method of looking at things that is rooted in Democritus's theory of atoms. Democritus had already envisioned all complex forms as consisting of elementary components of similar kind and as distinct only because of the different number and connection of those components. It was this idea that influenced decisively the interpretation of nature and modern science. Without this idea, the evolutionary theories, including that of living forms, would be no longer conceivable. This is completely different from the biblical conception of the sequence of created forms. Nevertheless, this is not sufficient to conclude the basic contradiction to the implicit intentions of the biblical report and of the idea of creation in general. There is no such contradiction as long as the contingency of each of the newly emerging forms is preserved, as is certainly the case in the doctrine of emergent evolution.

If the contingency of new forms is so important, the question must arise how contingency is to be reconciled to the peculiar logic suggested by the course of evolution moving in the direction from simple to more complex forms. Again and again philosophical and theological reflection on this phenomenon has arrived at the idea of some intrinsic teleological direction in the evolutionary process. The ideas of Pierre Teilhard de Chardin on this matter became widely known but also became the object of serious criticism.[16] Personally, I consider more plausible the vision of Michael Polanyi, who argues for the interpretation of the emergence of more or less durative forms of finite reality in terms of phases of equilibrium within the context of a field. He consequently perceives the evolutionary processes of ontogenesis as well as phylogenesis as field effects.[17] In this perspective, the evolutionary processes of phylogenesis and of ontogenesis are accounted for on the basis of determinants that are not only localized within the individuals in question or the genes as the models of sociobiology suggest today, but rather the future of the evolving forms is conceived as dependent on the overall status of a field that functions as the environment of individuals and species. Ideas of this kind that have been developed by Polanyi in more or less speculative ways are convergent with Alister Hardy's concept of "organic evolution." Furthermore, they do not only recommend themselves because they allow a description of organic and inorganic nature on the basis of the same fundamental conceptuality, but they also offer to the theologian a description of life processes in analogy to the biblical intuition of an origin of all life from the activity of the creative spirit of God.

Conclusion

In this chapter, I have suggested that the theologian cannot in good conscience simply accept as exhaustive the description of nature given us by the natural scientist. There is more to nature than simply what the scientist, working within the confines of the established disciplines, has been able to report. The reality of God is a factor in defining what nature is, and to ignore this fact leaves us with something less than a fully adequate explanation of things. The recognized contingency within natural events helps us perceive the contingency of nature's laws, and this cannot be accounted for apart from understanding the whole of nature as the creation of a free divine creator. The concept of the force field, both in terms of its historical antecedents and in terms of its systematic implications, needs careful assessment by the theologian. The concept of a field of force could be used to make effective our understanding of the spiritual presence of God in natural phenomena. Einstein's field theory comprises space, time, and energy in such a way as to make thinking about the whole of time intelligible. This, it seems, would give priority to eternity in our conception of time.

Our task as theologians is to relate to the natural sciences as they actually exist. We cannot create our own sciences. Yet we must go beyond what the sciences provide and include our understanding of God if we are properly to understand nature.

Notes

1. *D. Martin Luthers Werke*, Kritische Gesamtausgabe (Weimar, 1883), 4:4638 (entry no. 4638 of *Table Talk*, vol. 54 of *Luther's Works*, American Edition [Philadelphia: Fortress Press, 1967], 358–59.
2. Karl Gottlieb Bretschneider, *Handbuch der Dogmatik der evangelisch-lutherischen Kirche* (1814; 3d ed. 1828), 1:587.
3. Karl Barth, *Church Dogmatics*, 4 vols. (Edinburgh: T. & T. Clark, 1936–62), III/1, Preface.
4. Hans Blumenberg, *The Legitimacy of the Modern Age*, trans. Robert M. Wallace (Cambridge: MIT Press, 1983).

5. Alexandre Koyré, *Von der geschlossenen Welt zum unendlichen Universum* (Frankfurt: Suhrkamp Verlag, 1969), trans. from English, *From the Closed World to the Infinite Universe* (Baltimore: Johns Hopkins University Press, 1957), 163–64.

6. Max Jammer, *Concept of Force* (Cambridge: Harvard University Press, 1957).

7. William Berkson, *Fields of Force: The Development of a World View from Faraday to Einstein* (New York: John Wiley & Sons, 1974), 52ff.

8. Max Jammer, in *Historisches Wörterbuch der Philosophie*, ed. Joachim Ritter, 6 vols. (Basil: J. Ritter, 1971–84), 2:923.

9. Hermann Diels, *Die Fragmente der Vorsokratiker, griechisch und deutsch*, 3 vols. (Berlin: Weidmann, 1934–38), 13:B:2.

10. Berkson, *Fields of Force*, 317.

11. Ibid., 318.

12. Samuel Alexander, *Space, Time and Deity*, 2 vols. (London: Macmillan & Co., 1920), 1:39 n.1; cf. 147.

13. Plotinus, *Enneads* 3.7, 3, 16–17 and 2.7, 11.

14. Theodosius Dobzhansky, *The Biology of Ultimate Concern* (New York: New American Library, 1967), 33.

15. Edmund Schlink, *Ökumenische Dogmatik* (Göttingen: Vandenhoeck & Ruprecht, 1983), 93.

16. Pierre Teilhard de Chardin, *The Phenomenon of Man* (New York: Harper & Brothers, 1959).

17. Michael Polanyi, *Personal Knowledge: Towards a Post-Critical Philosophy*, 2d ed. (New York: Harper & Row 1962).

3

God and Nature

On the History of the Debates
Between Theology and Natural Science

The intellectual mind-set of the twentieth century has become accustomed to assuming that no relationship or connection can be
validly affirmed between the God of the Christian faith and the
understanding of the world in the natural sciences. The majority of
European Christian theologians of our century appear actually to
have considered this situation as an advantage, as an opportunity to
concentrate theology on the biblical revelation. This is exemplified
by Karl Barth's decision to refrain from any reference to scientific
insights and methods in the doctrine of creation of his *Church Dogmatics.*

Such a separation of the concept of God from questions about our
knowledge of nature also seems to support the modern philosophers
of religion who base speaking about God strictly on the subjectivity
of the human being. Characteristically, the arguments of modern
atheism from Feuerbach by way of Marx and Nietzsche to Freud,
Sartre, and Camus are directed likewise to the thematics of the self-
understanding of human beings and not to the problems of the
knowledge of nature. In looking in greater detail, however, one sees
that the restriction of the question concerning God to human beings
has its presupposition in modern thought, that is, in the development
of the mechanistic natural science of the eighteenth century, which
increasingly was separated from theological references. When the
scientific worldview became independent of the relationship with
God because of the purely mechanical description of the origin of
the planetary system in the pioneering work of Kant and Laplace—

although Kant himself was still motivated by a strictly Calvinistic understanding of God in transcendent majesty—only one approach to the reality of God was left open, namely, the contemplation of human self-consciousness and its foundations.

This approach was not new. It was known previously in ancient thinking and had found an intensively effective, classical representation in ancient Christianity, primarily in Augustine. But after Kant's critique of the proofs for the existence of God based on the understanding of the world, human self-understanding in modern philosophy has been considered, with few exceptions, as the only possible starting point for the elevation of thoughts to the idea of God—assuming that the attempt of a philosophical theology is made at all.

Perhaps the waning of philosophical theology in the philosophy of this century is also connected with that separation from the understanding of the world. One cannot think seriously of God—in any case, in the singular—without thinking of God as the origin of all that is and also of the origin of the world.[1] In actuality, nevertheless, Christian theology continues to speak of God as the creator of the world. Attempts at restricting the belief in creation to the existence of human beings have remained episodic. But the theological assurance that God is creator and lord of the world has become a doctrinal formula because the present worldview, which is oriented by the work of natural science and changes with its advances, has no internal relationship to the concept of God. The time of the blatant opposition to belief in God in the name of scientific progress has passed, in any case in the Western hemisphere. The blatant opposition has been replaced with a quiet and indifferent coexistence without relationship. This nonrelational coexistence is not necessary. There is taking place a narrow stream of philosophical-theological discussions with natural scientists in the Anglo-Saxon countries. In Germany, prominent scientists have repeatedly raised the question of God, not in the framework of their scientific research, but in their philosophical reflections. On the basis of the subject matter, occasions for developing a new relationship obviously exist and not only for the theologian. Thereby remarkable insights have been gained. However, they have not become known outside small circles, and it cannot be asserted that the heavy weights that would have to be moved have already begun to be rolled away.

My observations on this matter begin with a brief review of the main phases of the process up to the threshold of our century, a process that led to an estrangement between scientific and theological thinking. A subsidiary look will be directed at the separate developments in Great Britain and North America. It mainly concerns the attitude toward the theory of evolution. But it will be shown that the positive approaches to new contacts between the conception of nature and religion are in dire need of deepening, particularly in view of the idea of God itself. This will motivate us to return once more to the beginnings of the discussion on the relationship of the new natural science to the concept of God in order to take a closer look at certain ramifications.

The Copernican Revolution
and the Divorce of Nature and Theology

The first phase of the debate reaches back into the sixteenth century. It begins with the work of Copernicus. His heliocentrism and his doctrine of the motion of the earth around the sun, in contrast to the prevalent theory of its resting in place, were rejected not only by the Roman Church[2] but also by the Reformation. The Heidelberg historian of the Reformation, Heinrich Bornkamm, has described the complex processes concerning the publication of Copernicus's *De revolutionibus orbium coelestium* in Nuremberg in 1543, which was promoted under the authority of Melanchthon by Johann Rheticus and subsequently also by Andreas Osiander. Melanchthon was very much interested in astronomy and made pronouncements, particularly in his later years, not only critical but also with appreciation of the work of Copernicus. But he rejected Copernicus's theses as opposed to Holy Scripture. The issue was scriptural authority. Luther had commented in 1539 in a table talk on the rumors concerning the new astrologer who "wishes to turn the whole of astronomy upside down" (*totam astrologiam invertere vult*): he would rather believe the Holy Scriptures which report in the book of Joshua (10:12f.) that Joshua commanded the sun to stand still and not the earth (*tamen ego credo sacrae scripturae, nam Josua iussit solem stare, non terram*).[3] Otherwise Luther left the astronomical-astrological question to his friend Melanchthon, as he said in 1531: *Ego puto quod Philippus astrologica tractat, sicut ego bibo einen starken trunck birs, quando habeo graves cogitationes* (I believe that Philip deals with astrological matters, just as I take a strong drink of beer when I have grave thoughts).[4]

The rejection of the Copernican world system for the sake of the inspired authority of the Bible was retained in the Lutheran theology of Germany until the eighteenth century, contrary to England. David Hollaz, one of the last significant dogmaticians of old

Protestant orthodoxy before the invasion of Pietism and Enlightenment, considered the Copernican doctrine of the motion of the earth around the sun unacceptable as late as 1707 because it contradicted the scriptures.[5] After this writing, the situation also changed in Germany, as it had in England since the middle of the seventeenth century.[6] The well-educated Jena philosopher and theologian Johann Franz Buddeus avoided making explicit statements on the Copernican doctrine as late as 1724 in the doctrine of creation of his dogmatics. But he also did not oppose it and spoke, while treating the fourth day of creation, only incidentally of the "motion" of the sun and the moon as a standard for measuring time.[7] For the rest, he sought to offer an interpretation of the six-day work of creation according to the Genesis report which could be reconciled with the new natural science. The difficulty lay in the fact that the creation narrative assigns the emerging of sun and moon to the fourth day of creation, while the earth was created already on the third day. Buddeus took refuge in the idea that the creation of light on the first day of creation was already the production of a light-bearing body from which later the various heavenly bodies were shaped.[8] This idea is found also in the chief dogmatic work of German theology during the Enlightenment, the *Evangelische Glaubenslehre* by Siegmund Jakob Baumgarten (3 vols.), the first volume of which was published by his disciple J. S. Semler in 1759. Baumgarten interpreted the creation of light on the first day of creation in the sense of Descartes's theory of rotating vortices of particles. Out of the "collection" of fire and light particles, effected by it, came later the sun with other stars.[9] The later theology of the Enlightenment period recognized the division into days, just as other conceptions of the biblical report of the creation, as the expression of a cultic interest in the cosmological foundation of the consecration of the Sabbath[10] and as a description that corresponded to "the astronomical knowledge of that time." Therefore it is, thought Karl Gottlieb Bretschneider in 1814, "a lost effort to attempt to prove by physics the formations as told by Moses."[11]

The consequences, however, resulting from the new mechanical physics for the principal determination of the relationship of God to the world, became much more decisive for theology than the incompatibility of Copernicanism with the biblical creation narrative. Descartes, in his tract on the system of the world (*Le Monde*), written about 1630 but, for fear of the Inquisition, not published until 1664, after his death, had already asserted that God does not create order but a chaos from which order originates by itself.[12] Descartes's view is based on his formulation of the principle of inertia,[13] according to which each particle of matter remains in the condition in which it exists unless it is changed by external influences. This principle permitted one to describe all changes in the world as the result of the influences of the bodies on each other. Thus a recourse to God as the last originator of a motion was no longer necessary. Descartes's physics relied on the idea of God in order to lay a foundation for the principle of inertia itself: bodies are able to remain in their condition only because God immutably maintains the act of their creation and thus preserves them not only in their existence but also in their stage in each case. But the same immutability of God that lays the foundation for the preservation of the bodies in their stages prevented Descartes from attributing the changes in the world to God: they cannot be attributed to God, because the creative act of God does not change. Therefore all changes have to be attributed to nature, and their rules must be designated as laws of nature.[14] It is a presupposition for this that bodies move from the beginning and strive to continue their motion at any moment in a straight direction: in this way they are preserved by God at any moment. The influence of the bodies on each other causes the curvedness of their real motions, beginning with vortex motions out of which the stars originate.

The assumption that motion is proper to the bodies made the intervention of God into the natural processes seem superfluous and made possible their purely mechanical description. But the idea of the immutability of God also seemed to exclude such an intervention. Therefore it was entirely in agreement with the spirit of the physics of Descartes that Spinoza turned against the concept of miracle in his theological-political treatise published in Amsterdam in 1670. Spinoza made the question more precise by asking whether in nature anything could happen that is contradictory to its laws, and he answered with the remark that God then would have to contradict himself, because it was he who has given to nature its solid and immutable order in the laws of nature. Descartes's idea of the immutability of God is in the background. Spinoza combines it with the perfection of God. It would be unworthy of God if one were to assume that he "created Nature so ineffective and prescribed for her laws and rules so barren that he is often constrained to come to her rescue if he wants her to be preserved, and the course of events to be as he desires."[15] Thus from the perfection of God follows the perfection of his work which should not need any supplementary repairs.

This combination of the postulates of a purely mechanical explanation of nature as Descartes had demanded with the viewpoint of the perfection of the divine creator and his work, as it was expressed with special impressiveness in the metaphor of the perfect automatic clockwork, proved to be extremely influential also in theology. The critique of miracles by English deism was influenced by it just as much as was the German theology of the Enlightenment. Buddeus warned that those according to whom God had transferred, at the first act of creation, all further motions and shapings to matter and its laws separate God from the work of God's creation.[16] They even deny in truth the existence of God.[17] This clear-sighted warning was unable to prevail against this view. The philosopher Christian Wolff and the German theology of the Enlightenment following him sought to combine the mechanistic explanation of the world with the possibility of miracles by assuming that, on the one hand, the natural laws themselves are not necessary but contingent and that, on the other hand, the occurrence of miracles does not change the course of nature permanently.[18] Applied to the metaphor of the clockwork, Wolff compared the miracle with the advancing of the clock hand.[19] But even such a cautious and conservative theologian as Baumgarten saw himself forced to concede that God, only in a few extraordinary cases, for the sake of his gracious intention, transgresses the order given to nature, "since it would be a temptation of and offense against God to expect that God should effect by miracles and in an extraordinary way that which can be effected in order and according to the course of nature."[20] Baumgarten presupposed that the testimony of the scriptures makes the assumption of certain miracles necessary. Later historical-critical research attempted to show that even where scripture reports miracles, the same events might have occurred in one way or another quite naturally, whether the events only surpassed the comprehension of the people of the time or whether the reports have to be judged as products of myth-forming fantasy. It was demonstrated as an error of the theologians that they entered into a mediation of the normal preservation of the world by the mechanism of the natural context itself and attributed to God the role of a mere spectator. In any case, one did not pay the necessary attention to the concept of preservation while the immediate activity of God in the events of nature was limited to miracles.[21] The statements that Bretschneider wrote in 1828 on this subject sounded practically prophetic: "The deeper the knowledge of nature and of what is ordinarily found in nature advances, the more extensive is what we believe to derive from a law of nature; the more, therefore, the inclination decreases to see or to acknowledge the supernatural."[22]

Darwinian Evolution: Biological and Theological

The emancipation of nature from theology found its completion in the Darwinian theory of evolution. This theory was evaluated not only by the pioneers of a philosophical materialism but also by contemporary theology. Indeed, the theologians in the meantime had become more cautious and liked to emphasize that the Bible was not a scientific but a religious book.[23] But it was not yet admitted that with such an all too superficial explanation the biblical God is eliminated from the dispute concerning the understanding of the world. The leading Lutheran apologist of the time, the Leipzig professor C. E. Luthardt, assured his readers in his lectures, given in Leipzig in 1864, "Apologetische Vorträge über die Grundwahrheiten des Christentums," that the scripture in the progress of nature "toward human beings" sees "not only a natural development but a creative act of God."[24] Evidently, an alternative still existed for Luthardt: life itself, as well as its kinds and species, either emerges from an underivable creative act of God or is a product of a "development" from what already exists beforehand. In the discussions that took place in the following decades, up to the turn of the century, the opposition was even intensified: "Evolution or Revelation" was the title of the lecture given by the Greifswald dogmatician R. H. Grützmacher in Berlin in 1903. Other theologians, such as Max Reischle, made statements in a similar controversial vein.[25] The magisterium of the Roman Catholic Church had until 1950 taken a very distanced and rather negative position on the theory of evolution.

English and American theology, however, found, after initial vehement disputes,[26] more positive possibilities of interpreting the Christian faith suggested in the theory of evolution. Above all, Henry Drummond must be mentioned who, since his inaugural lecture in 1884 in Glasgow on "The Contribution of Science to Christianity," interpreted evolution as the way of God's creative activity toward the kingdom of God. Evolution, the concept of progress, and salvation history were here merged into a new total conception.[27] Since this view had several points of contact with the conceptions of the Greek church fathers of the divine economy of salvation, a circle of Anglican theologians was able to combine, in the collection *Lux Mundi*, edited by Charles Gore in 1889, the idea of evolution with a dynamic interpretation of the incarnation aiming at a new humanity. The theory of evolution was considered here practically as a liberation from the deterministic worldview of classical mechanics which had pushed God more and more out of the world. So Aubrey Moore wrote of Darwinism that in the disguise of an enemy it had shown itself actually as a friend of faith. It is only important to find God himself at work in the process of evolution.[28] This view of things has continued to have an effect on English and American theology. It reached its zenith in this century in the theological work of William Temple.

On the European continent, such ideas were promulgated in wide circles only by Pierre Teilhard de Chardin. Teilhard's option for the conception of an evolution toward an end, an orthogenesis, however, has given rise to critique. Even such an open-minded biologist as Adolf Portmann was impelled to declare it scientifically unacceptable.[29] Theological interpretations of evolution in England and North America, however, usually work with the concept of "emergent evolution," which became a formula of a worldview through the book of the same title by C. Lloyd Morgan (1923).[30] What is meant is that in the process of evolution something new appears in every step. Theodosius Dobzhansky, one of the noted biologists, who in recent times has contributed to the theological interpretation of evolution, says that evolution is "a source of novelty." Dobzhansky stresses the epigenetic character of evolution.[31] Alister Hardy, who by his concept of an "organic evolution" pays attention to modes of behavior as factors in selection, has also struggled for a relationship of religion and biology.[32] Charles Birch also must be counted in this group of theologizing biologists. In his book *Nature and God* (1965), Birch cites a poem by Lord Tennyson from the year 1850 that anticipates the combination of the theory of evolution and theology in almost Teilhardian tones:

> That God, which ever lives and loves,
> One God, one law, one element,
> And one far-off divine event,
> To which the whole creation moves.[33]

Indeed Tennyson was even less orthodox than Teilhard. The concept of God in his poem is obviously pantheistic. That cannot be said of most other theological interpretations of evolution. But among them also, the relationship of the idea of God and evolution is not really clarified. In most cases, God is imagined as a creative will who directs the process of evolution to its purpose.

The comprehensive presentation of the concept of a theology of evolution by the Cambridge biochemist and theologian Arthur Peacocke in his book *Creation and the World of Science* (1979) says explicitly that we must think of God as a "personal agent of the creative process" in analogy to the relationship of human consciousness to our body.[34] Peacocke is aware that this is a conception with a rich tradition. He himself mentions the key word "world soul" but remarks on it that he wishes to avoid a dualism of body and soul as it is at the basis of the traditional conception of soul. He also wants to avoid a pantheistic identification of the two. But the question of how God is to be thought, if both a metaphysical dualism and a monism are to be avoided, is answered for the reader only by saying that necessarily it is a question of "a higher order of transcendence than that of the human agent over his own actions."[35]

Newtonian Physics and Whiteheadian Metaphysics

This idea of God unavoidably contains conditions of human finitude, with the distinction of the subject of the action and the purpose of the action. In order to avoid the massive anthropomorphism of such an idea of God, other representatives of evolution-theological concepts have leaned on the process philosophy of Alfred North Whitehead. The problems connected with this cannot be discussed in detail here. Yet the philosophical theology of Whitehead seems to me to be subject to considerable misgivings, from the points of view both of theology and of philosophy of nature. From the point of view of theology, it must be said that Whitehead thinks of God only as one factor among others in the system of the universe, not as the creator of the world. From the point of view of the philosophy of nature, it seems unsatisfactory that space and time in Whitehead appear only as functions of the eventful "actual entities." Whitehead does not accept the conception of an ontologically original totality, perhaps in the sense of a field that has reality prior to particles and events and would be understood as the basis for their reality. Whitehead's system has, in these and in other points, much in common with Leibniz, namely, with his theory of monads and his conception of the ideality of space and time. Despite all the differences (among them: Leibniz in distinction from Whitehead thought of God as creator), it may be said that the contrast between Leibniz and Newton is repeated in the relationship of Whitehead's philosophy of nature to the metaphysical conceptions that historically lie at the basis of the field concept. This is the contrast between the conception of the reality of space as a condition for the reality of bodies and movements, on the one hand, and the reduction by Leibniz of space and time to invisible, punctiliar entities, the monads, on the other hand. Peacocke's conception of the relationship of God to the world in analogy to the relationship of soul and body is close to the Newtonian conception. Newton also wanted to be neither a dualist nor a pantheist. But he had more exact conceptions of the relationship of God to the world.

God and Space

Exactly these conceptions concerning the relationship of God and space were the subject of the famous controversy that was carried on in the years 1715 and 1716 between Leibniz and Samuel Clarke, Newton's theological friend and admirer.

This philosophical controversy became at the same time a contest for the judgment of a noble lady, Wilhelmine Charlotte, Princess of Wales, born in Ansbach. She admired Leibniz, who had conveyed to her a rather scornful opinion of Newton. Clarke, whom she met as a clergyman at court, now opposed this opinion, and she sent his exposition to Leibniz in order to hear his answer. Clarke wrote a reply to this answer which caused the princess to turn again for enlightenment to Leibniz. So it went back and forth for five times, with more and more detail added. Unfortunately the tone also became increasingly polemical. At the beginning, Leibniz had spoken to the princess about Newton rather condescendingly, and Clarke had at first defended Newton's conceptions in a restrained objectivity. But in his fourth and fifth replay, Clarke also gave way to insinuations and polemical exaggerations. Nevertheless, this controversy offers the fascinating picture of a philosophical debate that reveals more and more the ultimate foundations of two opposite positions that affected the future widely.

Leibniz had presented Newton to the princess as a half materialist who with his remark on space as the *sensorium Dei*, made in his *Opticks* in 1706, came close to the conception of God as a corporeal being. He also asserted that the inadequacy of Newton's conception of God is shown in the fact that Newton demotes the perfection of the divine work of creation as well as its creator by presenting the world as a machine constantly in need of repairs.[36] Clarke, whose replies must be considered an authentic interpretation of Newton,[37] answered to the first of these two points that Newton had used the concept *sensorium Dei* as a parable and that he understood it differently from what Leibniz thought.[38] But what concern stood behind these ideas of Newton? It is closely connected with the second question raised by Leibniz, with the seeming imperfection of a world machine dependent constantly for its renewal on an active intervention of God.

Alexandre Koyré has shown that Newton confronted with deep distrust the mechanical worldview of Descartes, which derived all change in the world alone from the mechanical mutual effects of the bodies. The Cartesian model of the world, in which the mutual play of mechanical powers was to explain the development from chaos to the ordered cosmos, seemed to him all too self-contained and self-sufficient so that it would not need any divine assistance or would even admit such. In his scientific papers, not published at the time, he uttered the fear that this worldview necessarily would lead to atheism.[39] This judgment agrees in an unexpected way with the scruples that theologians, such as the Jena dogmatician Johann Franz Buddeus, advocated in the following decades against a purely mechanical explanation of the world. The more interesting question, even from a theological viewpoint, is how Newton thought to catch this tendency of the mechanical explanation of nature, leading to a world independent from God. For this he used his theological interpretation of space as the form of the omnipresence of God with his creatures, an interpretation that was suggested by the English Platonist Henry More of Cambridge.[40] This indeed is the meaning of the designation of space as the *sensorium Dei*. Clarke has, in the sense of Newton, pointed out that *sensorium* is here not to be understood as the organ of perception—for this, God does not need a medium—but as the medium of the creation of the things: just as the sensorium in our perception creates the pictures of things, God through space creates the things themselves.[41]

How is this to be understood? In the famous *Scholium Generale* that Newton added in 1713 to the second edition of his chief work on the mathematical principles of the philosophy of nature, in order to clarify the relationship of his doctrines of physics to his religious and philosophical views, he says that God constitutes space and time through his eternity and omnipresence: "existendo semper et ubique, durationem et spatium constituit."[42] Leibniz misunderstood the expression *sensorium* as an organ of perception and obviously evaluated Clarke's explanations of it as an escape. Therefore he was also able to raise the objection that this conception makes God into a world soul.[43] But Newton had explicitly emphasized in his general scholium on the third book of the principles that God does not rule the universe as a world soul but as the Lord of all things.[44] Therefore he designates space as the effect of the presence of God with his creatures (see above). The expression *sensorium* indeed goes beyond this idea, because a sense organ, even when it is understood as the place of the production of its contents and not as the organ of their reception, cannot itself be a product of the perceiving individual.

Therefore Clarke has in his discussion with Leibniz designated absolute space as a property of God,[45] an expression that may be misunderstood because—as Leibniz objected—things may change their place in space so that space cannot be their property.[46] Space and the extension of this—in the case of God his *immensitas*—must be distinguished. Kant, in his *Critique of Pure Reason*, with his rejection of the conception of space as property, still seems to presuppose this argumentation of Leibniz.[47] After years of vacillation in his earlier writings on the philosophy of nature,[48] he finally followed the Leibniz conception of the subjectivity of space even if he conceived it, in distinction from Leibniz, as a form of perception. Leibniz, however, with his critique of the conception of space as property has not understood the idea that Clarke wanted to express by it. The reason seems to be that Leibniz thought of space with Descartes as a filled space and not as an empty space,[49] in which Kant, by the way, did not follow him. Newton and Clarke, however, thought of absolute space as empty, and this is decisive for their conception of the relationship of God and space. For Clarke, the conception of infinite space is implicit in the idea of the omnipresence or *immensitas* of God.[50] But it is implicit in it in the way that it has no divisions: infinite space is indeed divisible but not divided, and the conception of divisions always presupposes space.[51] On this basis it becomes understandable that space, on the one hand, could be designated as a *property* of God, or more exactly as an implication of the divine property of *immensitas*, but, on the other hand, as the *effect* of God, because by its divisibility it makes room for the finitude of the creatures.

Leibniz's critique missed this state of affairs because Leibniz—as mentioned—thought of space as already filled. Kant did not, but he followed the Leibniz rejection of the conception of space as attribute and the related thesis of the subjectivity of space, even though the bases for this truly had been eliminated with the assumption of the conception of empty space. If Kant had thematized the combination of the conception of empty space with the idea of God as it historically exists in Newton and Clarke,[52] he probably would not have so easily come to reduce the conception of space completely to human subjectivity. But Kant has, probably for reasons of his interest in the transcendence of God, which he saw rightfully denied by the nature piety of his age, hardly thought of a connection of God and space, not even in the sense of Newton's and Clarke's ideas of a constitution of space as an immediate implication or consequence of the divine *immensitas*. The turning away from the concept of infinity in Kant's statements about God and its supplanting by the thought of sublimeness is characteristic of it. For the idea of infinity, by way of *immensitas*, implies indeed omnipresence and eternity as infinity in space and time. The idea of absolute space follows immediately from the idea of God as Clarke had supported it in his debate with Leibniz and as the remarks of Newton, in his general scholium on the third book, indicate. But this means that this idea is independent from the manner in which Newton had introduced it in his physics by means of the law of inertia and the distinction between relative and absolute movement. Even if this physical foundation of absolute space in Newton has become unnecessary through the theory of relativity, the philosophical founding of the idea on the concept of God must not be affected by it. If Newton had indeed developed his doctrine of the mechanical kinds of motion only in order to prove the concept of absolute space, conceived previously for other reasons,[53] then it would be possible to question whether these philosophical-theological intentions do not have validity beyond the validity of his physical demonstration. The argument adduced by Clarke against Leibniz—that in all distinctions of parts the conception of space is already presupposed—is in any case independent of all alterations of physical theories. It is identical to the most important argument of Kant regarding the character in which space is viewed; and it could be capable of producing an immediate connection of the foundations of human experience with religious thematics. The idea of God beyond the element of infinity implies and constitutes exactly this conception of infinite space.

Does the idea of absolute, empty space as an expression of the omnipresence of God in Newton also fulfill the function that it should have according to the interpretation of Clarke and probably also in Newton's own understanding? This concerns the function of a correction of the system of natural processes which is governed by purely mechanical laws becoming independent vis-à-vis the creative and providential activity of God. According to Alexandre Koyré, Newton's *Scholium Generale* 1713 on the third book of the principles has to be read as an implicit rejection of Descartes's conception of God which, according to Newton, separated God from the world and made God absent from the world.[54] But God is present for the creatures through space, and "for Newton, it is just this presence that explains how God is able to move bodies in space by his will— just as we move our body by the command of our will."[55]

Space as the expression of the presence of God with creatures is, however, only the condition of God's continued activity in creation, not the proof of this activity itself. This proof required additional deliberations. Newton was of the opinion that the most important forces, especially that of gravity, are of a nonmechanical nature.[56] In his *Opticks* he wrote explicitly in 1706 that these "active principles" are derived directly from that powerful and immortal being who through omnipresence is able to move, shape, and renew all parts of the universe more easily than we are able to move by our will the members of our bodies.[57] In his *Opticks,* Newton emphasized beyond this that the order of nature becomes needful, in the course of time, of a renewal by God because as a result of the inertia of matter its irregularities increase.[58] The critique raised by Leibniz was directed against this thesis with special intensity, for it seemed to him to minimize the perfection of the creator himself by asserting the imperfection of his work. Clarke met this with the assertion: "The Notion of the World being a great *Machine* going on without the interposition of God as a clock continues to go without the assistance of a Clockmaker, is the Notion of Materialism and Fate and tends (under Pretense of making God a Super-Mundane Intelligence) to exclude Providence and God's Government in reality out of the World."[59] Leibniz defended himself against this accusation by averring that he did not doubt the necessity of the preservation of creation but only that of the correction of its order. But Clarke answered that one could speak of a correction only in view of our insight into nature by laws, but not in view of God's original plan for the world (Design), which includes from the beginning the appearance of disorder and the renovation following it.[60] The laws of nature ("the present Laws of motion") are, according to Clarke, expressed in today's terminology, only approximations to the real divine order of nature, which is historical and includes deterioration and renewal.

God and Time

Probably one must judge that in this dispute Newton and Clarke are closer to a theology of creation based on the Bible than Leibniz and Descartes. Even so, the relation of God to time, which Newton discussed only in connection with the viewpoint of *duration (der Dauer)*, could not find an appropriate clarification in the context of a mechanical theory of the events of nature. The relationship of the future of God to the emergence of what is new in the process of creation has been included in the consideration of the theology of nature only through the theory of evolution. The theological interpretation of evolution also has in many cases not yet advanced beyond the talk of a divine purpose, plan, or design, already found in

Clarke, to a differentiated discussion of the relationship of eternity and time under the viewpoint of their coincidence in the eschatological future of creation.

The greater proximity of Newton and Clarke to a biblically founded theology of creation appears in their emphasis on the continued activity of God in his creation. Leibniz had noticed this element only from the viewpoint of an order of grace, added to the order of nature. He considered the order of nature itself, for the sake of the perfection of the divine creator, independent from the need of the correcting interventions of God. This, however, laid a foundation for a complete separation of the understanding of nature from theology. More recent theology, primarily in Germany, has in these questions surrendered too uncritically to the influence of Leibniz, Wolff, and Kant. Kant also has, in the sense of Leibniz, understood his mechanical theory of the origin of the system of planets as an expression of the perfection of the divine work of creation which is not in need of any further intervention by its creator. A theology of a divine government of the world, oriented toward the history of salvation, could hardly be harmonized with this. Although the viewpoint of such a development was previously contained in this theory of Kant, it was not until the viewpoint of emergence, combined with the evolution of life, made again possible an interpretation of creation as a process directed by God's activity toward a future eschatological perfection.

A unique irony lies in the fact that Newton's physics became influential for the paradigm of the mechanical explanation of the world, the theological inadequacies of which he intended to overcome. The ensemble of classical theses of motion, founded on the principle of the self-preservation of motion, which Newton essentially had taken over from Descartes,[61] gained ground with its own weight against the ongoing intentions of Newton's philosophy of nature. With this in mind it is possible to see in overt attempts to counter the dominance of Newtonian mechanics, such as Faraday's field theory, an underlying renewal of the deeper intentions of Newton himself. However, Faraday, in seeking the unity of the nonbodily force which determines the natural processes but escapes mechanical description, was more inspired by Leibniz.[62] In a similar way perhaps the theory of relativity, with its elimination of the conceptions of the ether and of Newton's physical proofs for the absoluteness of space in connection with the principle of inertia, can be understood as a contribution to the revelation of the deeper theological intentions of Newton's philosophy of nature. For absolute space and absolute time, which the theory of relativity denies, were no

longer the absolute space and the absolute time of Newton conceived as the expression of the presence of God in creation. Metrical
systems of space and time, disassociated from the idea of God, will,
in the last analysis, show themselves as relative, also in the sense of
Newton's own distinction between relative and absolute motion, because only motion caused by God himself can be absolute.

Whether this applies to the speed of light will still have to be
demonstrated. In any case, the field concept, which Einstein put in
the place of the system of inertia of space-time and which, like other
fundamental concepts of physics, has, strictly speaking, not only a
function within the frame of physical theory but is at the same time,
on the basis of its origins, also a metaphysical category of the conception of nature, can be interpreted as an attempt to make precise
the intentions guiding Newton's philosophy of nature. This is the
case when, in the sense of Faraday, the total field of natural occurrences can be understood as a force field[63] appearing in the material
shapes as its singularities. Even the process of evolution could be
interpreted only in a frame of relationship comprehensively as an
expression of divine activity, present for the world process, without
surrendering an interpretation to the objection of a not sufficiently
mediated, almost occasionalistic introduction of the idea of God.

Conclusion: A Trinitarian Theology of Nature

Newton's thoughts on space and time as an expression of God's
presence with his creatures thus retain, without prejudice to the
corrections by modern physics of Newton's physical proofs for the
acceptance of absolute space, their significance for the philosophy of
nature and also for a modern theology of nature. The examination
of the arguments directed against them by Leibniz and others is a
necessary task in the frame of the critical revision of Cartesian dualism of spirit and body. This does not mean that, alongside physical
criticisms of Newton's thesis of space, objections should not be
lodged against Newton's theological conception. Newton's theology
was not pantheistic, as was thought, but it had also no relationship
to the doctrine of the Trinity. Today's Christian theology of creation
will use, in distinction from Newton, the possibilities of the doctrine
of the Trinity in order to describe the relationship of God's transcendence and immanence in creation and in the history of salvation.
Perhaps a renewed doctrine of the Trinity would combine the Logos
doctrine of the ancient church with contemporary information
theory and recognize the activity of the divine spirit in the self-

transcendence of life and its evolution. Only a Trinitarian theology is able to meet effectively the emancipation of the concept of the world that Newton had in mind—that is, the mechanical description of nature that is not only a theoretical construction but takes place in the actual processes of the world itself. A Christian theology of creation will be able to develop a description that does justice to this emancipation of the world process and at the same time removes its disassociation from its divine origin only by way of the theology of the Trinity, in a perspective of the history of salvation. In this way it will also cope with the critique of Leibniz insofar as Newton's idea of God was not commensurate with this task. However, a theology of nature must not go back behind Newton's thought on the presence of God with his creatures through space and time, if theology is to avoid the spell of a powerless dualism of spirit and matter.

Notes

1. See W. H. Austin, *The Relevance of Natural Science to Theology* (London: Macmillan & Co., 1976), 57ff.
2. The first trial of Galileo was in 1616. The prohibition of the work of Copernicus was lifted in 1757; and the judgment against Galileo's *Dialogues* of 1632 dealing with the opposition between the new and old world systems was first lifted in 1822. Cf. A. D. White, *A History of the Warfare of Science with Theology in Christendom*, 2 vols. (1896; repr. New York: Dover Publications, 1960), 1:158ff.
3. WA.TR IV, no. 4638 = *Luther's Works*, American Edition (Minneapolis: Fortress Press, 1967), vol. 54, *Table Talk*, 358f. Cf. on the whole matter, Heinrich Bornkamm, "Kopernikus im Urteil der Reformatoren," *Archiv für Reformationsgeschichte* 40 (1943): 171–83; and Hans Blumenberg, *Die kopernikanische Wende* (Frankfurt, 1965), 100–21.
4. WA.TR EA 57, no. 17, cited according to Blumenberg, *Die kopernikanische Wende*, 173.
5. D. Hollaz, *Examen Theologicum Acroamaticum* (1707; reprint 1971), 539f. On further pronouncements of old Protestant theologians of the seventeenth century, see J. Dillenberger, *Protestant Thought and Natural Science: A Historical Interpretation of the Issues Behind the 500-Year-Old Debate* (New York: Doubleday & Co., 1960), 93ff. See ibid., p. 101, on the Cartesian theologians in the Netherlands.
6. See Dillenberger, *Protestant Thought*, 105f.
7. J. F. Buddeus, *Compendium Institutionum Theologiae Dogmaticae* (Leipzig, 1724), 225.
8. Ibid., 219.
9. Siegmund Jakob Baumgarten, *Evangelische Glaubenslehre*, 2d ed. (Halle, 1764), 1:616 and 623f.
10. Thus first J. G. Töllner, "Die Schöpfungsgeschichte," in *Theologische Untersuchungen* I, 2 (1773): 325–52. The interpretation of the biblical

primeval history as an expression of a worldview schema which is passé for the present was brought to prominence in theology primarily by the *Urgeschichte* of J. G. Eichhorn, which appeared for the first time in 1779 and was later edited by J. P. Gabler in three volumes in 1790–93.

11. Karl Gottlieb Bretschneider, *Handbuch der Dogmatik der evangelisch-lutherischen Kirche* (1814; 3d ed. 1828), 1:598 and 597. Bretschneider here turns against the attempt, made by Franz Volkmar Reinhard in his lectures on dogmatics in 1801 (pp. 169ff.), to understand the statement of the creation narrative "not as referring to the emerging and formation of the entire world but only to the formation of the earth" (ibid., p. 170; cf. p. 172), in order to be able to prove in this way also its physical correctness.

12. René Descartes, *Oeuvres,* ed. Charles Adam and Paul Tannery, 7 vols. (Paris), 11 (1967), 34.

13. Ibid., 38. Here the new concept of the status (*estat*) of a body is decisive which is superior to the distinction of rest and movement (p. 40). Against the traditional (Aristotelian) view, according to which each body strives on its own toward the state of rest, so that any movement has to come from the outside, Descartes objects that movement then would have to endeavor to destroy itself, in contrast to all other things that strive to preserve themselves (p. 40, I. 14ff.). Cf. also Descartes's *Principia philosophiae* 2.41 (Adam/Tannery, 8/1 [1964], 65f.). On the conception of the principle of inertia in Descartes and its significance for Newton, cf. Alexandre Koyré, *Newtonian Studies* (Cambridge: Harvard University Press, 1965), 66ff., 70ff. On the prehistory of the conception developed in *Le Monde,* idem, *Galileo Studies* (French, 1939; Hassocks, 1978), 79ff., and on the conception itself, pp. 251–66.

14. Because the bodies influence each other, it follows "qu'il doit y avoir plusieurs changemens en ses parties, lesquel ne pouvant, ce me semble, être proprement attribuez à l'action de Dieu, parce qu'elle ne change point, je les attribue à la Nature; et les règles suivant lesquelles se font ces changemens, je les nomme les Loix de la Nature" (Adam/Tannery, 11:35, I. 5ff.).

15. Baruch Spinoza, *Tractatus Theologico-Politicus* (1670), trans. S. Shirley ch. 6 (Leiden: E. J. Brill, 1989), 126.

16. Buddeus (see above, n. 7), 216: "Non minus tamen et illi ultra quam decet sapiunt qui, posita materia, motuque, et huius certis legibus, cuncta in istam quam hodie conspicimus formam per solas istas naturae leges disponi, ac produci potuisse, aut omnino disposita ac producta esse contendunt, creationem in naturalem quandam generationem commutantes, immo, hoc agentes, ut Deum sensim ab opere creationis removeant, mundumque et sine Deo fieri potuisse sibi aliisque persuadeant." Later (p. 299), Buddeus identified this point of view expressly as the explanation of the world by the *mechanica ratio* of the laws of motion.

17. Ibid., 286: Those who (explain) the preservation of things by the creator "ita explicant, quod Deus in prima creatione rebus eiusmodi vim operandi concesserit, revera eum negant."

18. Christian Wolff, *Cosmologia Generalis,* § 514ff., esp. § 527 and 574ff. (*Werke,* ed. J. Ecole II, 4 [1964], 398ff., 410f., 445ff.). This thesis is the

more remarkable as Wolff contrasted the miracle, according to its concept, with the course of nature (*contra cursum naturae:* § 568, p. 441), and did not understand it with Spinoza and Locke only as an event that exceeds the comprehension of the contemporaries (§ 514, pp. 398f.).

19. Ibid., § 534 (pp. 417f.).
20. Baumgarten, *Evangelische Glaubenslehre,* 1:845 (*β*).
21. Bretschneider, *Handbuch der Dogmatik,* 607. In making the natural context independent, one makes "God an idle spectator of the world" (p. 124) and leads to the circumstance "that one finally drives God completely out of nature, i.e., makes him a dead idol" (p. 122). Cf. p. 125.
22. Ibid., 122. Bretschneider, however, wishes to have "the ordinary, the analogous in the becoming of the things" in the same way related to God's activity as the extraordinary (pp. 122f.). But evidently he was not clear that more is necessary for this to happen than a theological declaration of intention, namely, a different understanding of nature than that of classical mechanics.
23. Christoph Ernst Luthardt, *Apologetische Vorträge über die Grundwahrheiten des Christentums* (1864; 11th ed. 1889), 1:84.
24. Ibid., 95. Cf. 311ff. See also the explications of K. H. A. Ebrard, *Apologetik: Wissenschaftliche Rechtfertigung des Christentums* (1874), 1:347–97.
25. References in E. Benz, *Schöpfungsglaube und Endzeiterwartung* (Munich, 1965), 113ff.
26. On the appearance of Bishop S. Wilberforce in the British Society in Oxford on June 30, 1860, cf. Benz, *Schöpfungsglaube;* and especially R. H. Overman, *Evolution and the Christian Doctrine of Creation: A Whiteheadian Interpretation* (Philadelphia: Westminster Press, 1967), 72ff.
27. Dillenberger, *Protestant Thought,* 247. See also Overman, *Evolution,* 79ff.
28. *Lux Mundi,* 73, cited by Overman, *Evolution,* 79ff.
29. Adolf Portmann, *Der Pfeil des Humanen* (Freiburg, 1960), 26ff. and 41ff.
30. On C. Lloyd Morgan and the related views of Samuel Alexander, see the presentation by Eric C. Rust, *Evolutionary Philosophies and Contemporary Theology* (Philadelphia: Westminster Press, 1969), 77ff.
31. Theodosius Dobzhansky, *The Biology of Ultimate Concern* (New York: New American Library, 1967), 33. On what follows, see p. 29. The significance of this viewpoint for the dialogue between theology and the theory of evolution had been emphasized in 1909 by the Erlangen theologian Karl Beth (*Der Entwicklungsgedanke und das Christentum*). But Beth's ideas have not had a notable effect in Germany.
32. Alister Hardy, *The Biology of God: A Scientist's Study of Man the Religious Animal* (London: J. Cape, 1975); German title, *Der Mensch—das betende Tier* (Stuttgart, 1979).
33. From Alfred, Lord Tennyson, *In Memoriam,* cited by Louis Charles Birch, *Nature and God* (London: SCM Press, 1965; Philadelphia: Westminster Press; 1966), 28.
34. A. R. Peacocke, *Creation and the World of Science* (Oxford: Clarendon

Press, 1979), 134 (on the key word "personal agent," see pp. 199 and 41ff.). See also R. W. Burhoe, *Toward a Scientific Theology: Essays on the Relation of Science to Religion* (Belfast: Christian Journals, 1980), 116ff.

35. Peacocke, *Creation,* 138f.; quotation on 139.

36. G. W. Leibniz, *Die philosophischen Schriften,* ed. C. J. Gerhardt, 7 vols. (1875–90), 7:352. The replies of Clarke also are printed in this volume. Alexandre Koyré, *Von der geschlossenen Welt zum unendlichen Universum* (Eng., 1957; Ger., Frankfurt: Suhrkamp Verlag, 1969), 211–45, offers a survey of the controversy between Leibniz and Clarke.

37. Thus Koyré, *Geschlossene Welt,* 213 n. (3), and idem, with I. Bernard Cohen, in *AThS* 15 (1962): 63–126.

38. Gerhardt, 7:353. See on this the explanations of Koyré, *Newtonian Studies,* 109f. n. 3.

39. Koyré, *Newtonian Studies,* 93f.

40. On Henry More, see E. A. Burtt, *The Metaphysical Foundations of Modern Physical Science* (1925; rev. ed., New York: Doubleday & Co., Anchor Books, 1937), 135–50; further, Koyré, *Geschlossene Welt,* 105–43; and on his influence on Newton, ibid., 147ff. See further Max Jammer, *Das Problem des Raumes: Die Entwicklung der Raumtheorien* (Darmstadt: Wissenschaftliche Buchgesellschaft, 1960), 41ff. and 118ff.

41. Gerhardt, 7:353: "Sir Isaac Newton considers the Brain and Organs of Sensation, as the Means by which those Pictures are formed, but not as the Means by which the Mind sees or perceives those pictures, when they are so formed."

42. Isaac Newton, *Philosophiae Naturalis Principia Mathematica, 3d ed. (1726): With variant readings assembled and edited by Alexandre Koyré and I. Bernard Cohen,* 2 vols. (Cambridge: Harvard University Press, 1972), II, 761 (528, 25f.). Jammer does not present this statement correctly when he says that Newton here "equates space and time with the attributes of God" (p. 121). Rather, space is "constituted" by the divine omnipresence so that it is the effect of the latter.

43. Gerhardt, 7:375.

44. See above, n. 42, II, 760 (528, 1f.): "Hic omnia regit non ut anima mundi, sed ut universorum dominus."

45. Gerhardt, 7:368 n. 3: "Space is not a Being, an eternal and infinite Being, but a Property, or a consequence of the Existence of a Being infinite and eternal. *Infinite Space is Immensity.*" Clarke answered here Leibniz's remark that the conception of space as real and absolute leads to great difficulties: "Car il paroist que cet Etre doit être Eternel et infini" (p. 363 n. 3).

46. Gerhardt, 7:398: "Si l'Espace est une proprieté et si l'espace infini est l'immensité de Dieu . . . l'espace fini sera l'étendue ou la mensurabilité de quelque chose finie. Ainsi l'espace occupé par un corps, sera l'étendue de ce corps: chose absurde, puisqu'un peut changer d'espace, mais il ne peut point quitter son étendue." Still less can *empty* space be conceived as property according to Leibniz; for to what substance would it then belong (as its extension) (ibid., 372f. nn. 8 and 9)?

47. On the *Critique of Pure Reason* (1781), A 26 ("Space does not constitute a property of any kind of things in themselves or in their relation with each other"), see H. Vaihinger, *Kommentar zu Kants Kritik der reinen Vernunft* (1881), 2:133.

48. See Jammer, *Das Problem des Raumes*, 142ff.
49. Gerhardt, 7:364 n. 5: "Sans des choses y placées, un point de l'espace ne diffère absolument en rien d'un autre point de l'espace." Therefore, space is for Leibniz only the form of order and of the relations of things (*un ordre de Coexistances*, ibid., 363 n. 4). In the same manner, the moments of time are nothing without the things and their sequence (p. 364 n. 6). The conception of an empty space (or an empty time) is therefore imaginary (p. 372 n. 7). But there is no emptiness in nature, for this would violate, according to Leibniz, the principle of sufficient ground (p. 378).
50. See above, n. 43. Cf. p. 383 n. 10: "Space and Duration are not hors de Dieu, but are *caused by* and are immediate and necessary Consequences of His existence: And *without* them, His eternity and ubiquity (or Omnipresence) would be taken away." Conversely, space as empty space cannot belong to a body: "Space void of Body, is the Property of an *incorporeal* Substance" (ibid.).
51. Gerhardt, 7:383 nn. 11ff.: Space is divisible but composed of parts only in our conception. Leibniz had argued for his critique of the combination of infinite space with the concept of God in this way: "Mais comme il a des parties, ce n'est pas une chose qui puisse convenier à Dieu" (p. 363 n. 3). Clarke had answered to this: "Nor is there any Difficulty in what is here alleged about Space having Parts. For *Infinite Space is one*, absolutely and *essentially indivisible*: And to suppose it parted, is a contradiction in Terms; because there must be Space in the Partition itself; which is to suppose it *parted,* and yet *not parted* at the same time" (p. 368 n. 3). Leibniz considered this complete nonsense (p. 373 n. 11).
52. According to Kant, the conception of space is characterized by the fact that space as an infinite unit ("an infinite *given* entity": *Critique of Pure Reason,* B 39f.) always underlies all conceptions of parts of space, entirely in line with the argumentation of Clarke (see above, n. 51). Should the conception of space then not always already imply the elevation to the infinity (as first approximation to the idea of God) which becomes the theme in Kant's systematics of pure reason only at a much later place? In his *Critique of Judgment,* Kant comes close to this state of affairs under the concept of the Mathematically Sublime (§ 25ff.) but discusses it only in view of "things of nature" and not in view of the underlying conception of space itself, therefore also only under the viewpoint of subsequent reflection and not under that already of an implication of the original conception of space. But perhaps the suppression of the concept of the infinite in Kant's conception of God by the concept of all-sufficiency (since 1763) can contribute to an explication of this viewpoint which is curious in view of the piety of nature of the young Kant (cf. H. G. Redmann, *Gott und Welt: Die Schöpfungstheologie der vorkritischen Periode Kants* [Göttingen: Vandenhoeck & Ruprecht, 1962], esp. pp. 68f. and the quotations on p. 60 from the *Allgemeinen Naturgeschichte und Theorie des Himmels.* The fact that Redmann speaks of a "pantheizing piety of nature of Newton" from which he would like to distinguish the statements of Kant [p. 61] is in need of correction because in this way the conception of Newton itself is misunderstood).

53. Thus Jammer, *Das Problem des Raumes*, 125.
54. Koyré, *Newtonian Studies*, 112.
55. Ibid., 91.
56. Ibid., 109.
57. Isaac Newton, *Opticks* (New York: Dover Publications, 1952), qu. 31 and 28 (pp. 403 and 370).
58. Cf. Burtt, *Metaphysical Foundations*, 295f.
59. Gerhardt, 7:354.
60. Ibid., 361 n. 8. Cf. Leibniz, ibid., 358.
61. See Koyré, *Newtonian Studies*, 66ff., 70ff.
62. Thus William Berkson, *Fields of Force: The Development of a World View from Faraday to Einstein* (New York: John Wiley & Sons, 1974), 31, 39ff., 50f.
63. Ibid., 324f.; cf. 317f.

4

Contingency
and Natural Law

Can there be at all something like a theology of nature? It is not only skepticism informed by natural science which opposes any attempt of this kind. From the point of view of theology one may also pose this question only with suspicion and disquiet. Does not theology have to speak of "creation" where other sciences use the word "nature"? Is this terminological difference not a sign of the segregation of theological thinking that separates it from the natural sciences and of all philosophy of nature? But whatever the issue of such a segregated particularity may be, it should not serve as a pretense to make acceptable the chasm between theology and knowledge of nature, a chasm that for centuries has constantly widened and today seems often unbridgeable. If the one God of the Christian faith is also the Lord of nature, then we will not be satisfied with this chasm. Therefore it is amiss if already in setting the theme of creation we produce a separation.

Therefore the fundamental task of theology in this case is better characterized as a "theology of nature." With this, the concept of "creation" is by no means surrendered. It designates a possible result of a theology of nature, of a theological interpretation of natural reality. However, it is not to be taken for granted that the theological conversation concerning nature leads to this result. From many aspects, the word "creation," or in any case its usual understanding, is not very appropriate for a theology of nature. It is especially amiss that at the word "creation" people think often only, or in any case in the first instance, of the beginning of the world. A theology of nature, in contrast, would have to address nature in its entire process and in its present circumstance, including its beginning history. It would have to relate all of nature to the reality that is the true theme of theology—the reality of God. In this sense, the term "creation" would have to be defined anew if it is to be suitable as the main concept for the subject of a theology of nature.[1]

The Feasibility of a Theology of Nature

The feasibility of a theology of nature is challenged by theological suspicion, and it is challenged even more by the skepticism arising from the natural sciences. Did not the modern understanding of nature originate exactly in the process of its emancipation from theology? How, then, can a theology of nature be possible that does not speak immediately of something quite different from nature as it is understood in the research of the natural sciences?

It cannot be denied that the history of modern natural science to a great deal has been a history of the emancipation of science from theological presuppositions. The Aristotelianism of the Middle Ages and especially the thinkers influenced by Averroës still saw it as a specific task of physics to lay a foundation for the concept of God. In modern times, however, theology has been expelled from physics step by step.[2] At first, the constant intervention of God into the events of the cosmos became superfluous, and the relationship of God to the world was restricted to the explanation of its beginnings. Thus it received deistic features: God appeared as the engineer of the world as a whole who, after the completion of this work, went into retirement. To expect something from God for the present life, for example, an action that would transform the world, seemed irreconcilable with this concept. Therefore it is understandable that Christian theology, which lives from a conception of salvation, could not be pleased with such a deistic view. But then its apologetic need seemed to have been satisfied with the gaps in the explanation of nature, with the apparent leaps at the transition from lower to higher levels. The victorious march of the theory of evolution eventually expelled theology from these bastions. The connections that combine the beginnings of humanity with the evolution of life and the beginnings of life with highly complicated inorganic structures have become closer and closer.

The chain of defeats of theological apologetics by the natural sciences makes it understandable that the caution of theologians, who no longer want to burn their fingers, has been increasing in the last decades. Nevertheless, theology must not become prey to the all too comfortable escape to the idea of creation on a special or exclusively theological level which is inaccessible to any critique by the natural sciences, for example, as an interpretation of the first two chapters of the Bible.[3] This protection from critique by the natural sciences signifies at the same time the irrelevancy of theological statements, not only for the work of the natural scientist but also for the worldview of today's humanity which is rightfully informed by the results of the natural sciences. Exactly that nature which is researched by natural science would have to be claimed by theology as the creation of God. Not even a conception of the doctrine of creation that is reduced to that which is existential provides an escape from this difficulty. The conviction that God has created "me"[4] cannot serve as a foundation of a doctrine of creation that is sure in itself. In view of the indubitable embedding of the individual into the phylogenetic process of humanity and thus into the events of all of nature, the assertion that God has created "me" remains an emotional exaggeration unless other reasons than the subjective feeling of finiteness urge us to bring natural events into connection with the question of God. The confession of the God of the Christian message as the creator of heaven and earth remains empty, remains a mere confession of the lips, as long as one cannot affirm with good reasons that nature, with which the natural scientist is concerned, has something to do with this God.[5] Immense significance would be attached to such a proof or its failure, especially for the present debate concerning the idea of God itself. To be sure, the idea of God can for modern human beings no longer be founded on the knowledge of nature. It is more likely that anthropology would be the soil on which the function of the idea of God for the human understanding of reality is to be investigated and reasons for its justification are to be sought. Only here can the objection be met that the idea of God is a fiction of human beings, to be derived from certain motives. But even with a rejection of this suspicion nothing yet would have been decided about the reality of God. Rather, this decision is made in the connection of the whole human experience of the world and the self. In this frame, the knowledge of nature also retains its relevancy for the idea of God.

The actual conception of the whole of reality and the experiences that modify it are the field of the specifically religious life. Religion is not necessarily based on a marginal and obscure special experience; rather, it is concerned with the experience of the power that determines the reality of being as a whole, which transcends as such all special, isolatable and disposable powers and strengths. Its manifestation in certain concrete events gives them the character of religious experience. Since such religious experience is an aspect of human behavior, its interpretation and evaluation have to enter into general anthropological questions. However, its truth cannot be decided on this basis alone. The affirmation of divine reality, rather, can be justified only on the condition that the affirmed reality can be understood as the origin of all that is real, that is, also of nature and its possible consummation. Nature here is nature as we have to see it today, namely, as in the field of modern natural science. A God who would not be the origin and perfecter of this nature could not be the power that determines all reality of being, and therefore not truly God. If theology wants to think of the deity of God, then it has to think of God as the power that determines not only human history but also nature. This demand results in addition from the observation that in human history itself events proceed only naturally; so, either history and nature together or neither one has anything to do with God.

Mere theological assurances of the power of God over nature, however, remain insufficient, since, at least in appearance, the reality of human life in a world that is affected by natural science contradicts a divine power over nature totally. How can one speak of a supposedly all-determinative power if its denial does not bring any disadvantages at all for the knowledge and technical control of the natural processes but, on the contrary, has even enabled human beings to proclaim themselves masters of nature?[6] It is not without penalty that theology has turned away from the task of a theological permeation and digestion of the scientific thinking of modern times. In this way, understanding of nature has been alienated from its original starting points which were at least partially motivated by Christianity. This has created an atmosphere that may present today the renunciation of Christian eschatology, of the message of Jesus' resurrection, even of the idea of God itself as a demand of intellectual honesty.

Despite the great works of Karl Beth (1908/10) and Arthur Titius (1926), there was a widespread inclination of theological indolence to evade the debate with scientific thinking and to recommend such an evasion even as an especially pure expression of Christian orthodoxy. Therefore the effort of the grandly planned investigations of Karl Heim[7] to relate theological and scientific questionings and results with each other have to be commended as pioneering.

However, Heim often connected the two realms only by a figurative transfer of scientifically defined concepts to theological problems. Even the concept of dimension is probably used only figuratively when Heim related the realm of theological statements as a new dimension, as the dimension of the "suprapolar," to the dimension of the scientific space-time world.[8] The binding force of such a supplement for the natural scientist, even if only for his or her philosophical self-understanding, remained unexplained.

This lack in the efforts of Heim makes the task clear to which the following deliberations are dedicated: a common ground is to be sought to which scientific and theological problematics can be referred without losing sight of the specific difference of the two ways of thinking. In what follows, I make the attempt to sketch such a common ground in a preparatory way. It is designated by the relation of contingency and regularity.

Contingency and the Biblical View of God

On the basis of the Israelite understanding of God, which has influenced early Christianity also, the experience of reality is characterized primarily by contingency,[9] particularly contingency of occurrences.[10] New and unforeseen events take place constantly that are experienced as the work of almighty God. Therefore not only this or that individual happening but all occurrences are basically miraculous or wonderful. Only on the presupposition of such an understanding of reality is it meaningful, for the Israelite and for the Christian heir of the Israelite tradition, to pray. Furthermore, on this basis faith appears as the behavior that is, in the last analysis, alone appropriate to reality. For the fact that again and again new events take place means that one cannot render a final judgment concerning the context in which present and past events and figures stand and from which their significance is to be determined: only the future will reveal what is "in it."

An understanding of nature in the sign of such contingency[11] stands apparently in fundamental contrast to the question of an unbreakable order in the natural events, in contrast to the Greek conception of the cosmos and in contrast as well to the understanding of classical modern science regarding the thoroughgoing regularity of nature. It is true that even Israelite thinking, as it is preserved in the writings of the Old Testament, was aware of permanent orders in nature as well as in human society. But these orders were conceived as dependent on the contingency of the divine will, not only in view of their origin but also in view of their continuance. Nature's regularities can be compared with positive legislation, whose laws fundamentally permit of exceptions and can be changed by the legislator, rather than with the idea of a law of nature that permits of no exceptions and is unchangeable.[12] In the period of classical physics, it seemed that the quest for laws of nature in this sense progressively excludes accidents within the course of the world—that is, apart from the unavoidable contingency of the conditions at the beginning. Indeed, the course of classical physics was widely determined by faith in an eternal order of the universe, in view of which everything contingent had to be considered as something that only seemed to be so preliminarily, which was not yet recognized in its regular order that is to be presupposed. That which is accidental was not judged positively as something contingent in each case, but only negatively as something that is not yet perceived in its necessity. An accident belongs to that which is inessential.

Since this view of things led to such impressive results, the question suggests itself whether the biblical understanding of reality in the sign of the contingency of occurrences, which was interpreted as divine action, does not rest on an illusion. Are not all events determined by eternal laws, so that only naive experience would speak of accidents? Modernity has believed for a long time that this is so. Therefore the understanding of reality that is common to the biblical writings—the understanding of all events as contingent occurrences with all variation in details which agrees essentially with the biblical concept of God—had to be considered as unbelievable and abolished.

Probably it is seen today more clearly than was possible in the nineteenth century that a sort of religious faith, a late form of Greek cosmos piety, played a role in the deterministic worldview of classical natural science. That determinism is an illusion may have been revealed by contemporary physics insofar as the latter has produced a more realistic consciousness of the limits of physical and scientific laws as such. This sobering up with regard to the significance of physical awareness of laws for a worldview, however, is grounded in the particular results of quantum physics, even if occasioned by them. In principle it was possible even in the golden age of classical physics[13] to be conscious of the limits that are imposed on questions of physics for connections in terms of laws of nature, not from the outside but by its own essence. This was possible when it was not opposed by a faith in the thoroughgoing determinedness of all natural occurrences by laws, known and still unknown, which are always alike. Today this faith is shattered. The micro structure of natural events can be described only by statements of probability, and this obviously not because of the limitedness of present physical knowledge but because of the nature of the matter itself. Furthermore, it seems that a certain preliminariness belongs to the formulation of the laws of nature: when new observations make it necessary, formulas previously considered as constantly valid will have to be considered as mere approximations of more general regularities.[14] Thus the possibility exists that the laws of nature that are today familiar to humanity are limited in time and space in their field of application, so that they do not have to be applicable in every former or future time and not everywhere in the same way. If the process of the universe has the character of a unique and irreversible total process, then a temporal limitation in the applicability of formulas of the laws of nature may be more than merely conceivable.

In reflecting on the limitation of regularity by the contingency of natural events, the issue cannot be to discover this or that gap in the regular explanation of events.[15] Today's theology considers it hardly enticing to win proofs for the existence of God from gaps in the natural events, "as if God would fill only the gaps in the natural process which otherwise is automatic and would not instead be the creator of the whole world process."[16] According to experience, such gaps are being closed ever anew by progressive research in natural science. Therefore one should not put too much weight on the fact that, for example, the origin of life from inorganic processes is physically inconceivable.[17] Why shall it remain inconceivable in the future? There is basically no question in physics for which a physical answer—if any at all—would not be possible.[18] It only can be assumed that with each new result new problems also come about.

The question of the relationship of contingency and regularity seems to be posed in a constantly new form. The contingency of events becomes prominent for every status of research in special points in each case, for us today not only in microphysics but also with the problems of turbulent movement. These problems are significant for the questions of the origin of the universe and the history of stars. Contingency is important also in view of the origin of life and the processes of mutation in the process of the development of species. The points where the contingency of natural events is especially weighty may shift in the process of research. Yet in every new stage of research, the total process of natural events presents itself again as a mesh of contingency and regularities.[19] Thereby natural science pursues thematically the aspect of regularity, the regular connections in the occurrences. But can it ever succeed in bringing into view the entirety of nature as determined in all details by a number of laws that are in any case not infinitely complex? This would mean at the same time that a stage of research is conceivable from which nothing more could be discovered. Many natural scientists have had this nightmare because of the successes of their own research. Fortunately it probably is not a truthful dream. Laws always uncover what is necessary superimposed on what is contingent. This is the substratum of the knowledge of law itself. From this follows the "inexhaustibility of reality by individual insights into its structure."[20]

Have we reached, with contingency and regularity, a final, irreducible antagonism in the contemplation of nature? Or is a viewpoint conceivable that unites these two aspects? If the contingency of occurrences cannot be dissolved into a progressively differentiated system of connections of laws of nature, can perhaps, on the contrary, the contingent occurrences be conceived as comprising the regularity of nature? Can the regular events, or rather the forms of events that can be described by assertions of regularity, perhaps themselves be conceived of as a class of contingent events? This question, of course, cannot have the aim of deriving regularity from the *concept* of contingency. Such a demand would be absurd. Rather, the question is meant ontologically: do the contingent occurrences let us recognize in their special character as occurrences, which is to be more closely investigated, regularity as their own element in such a way that the presence of regularity can be thought together with the contingency of occurrences, not only under abstraction from the contingency of occurrences?

Perhaps the task of the confirmation of the biblical idea of God can today be formulated in this way with reference to the entirety of reality in view of the understanding of nature. The general form of this task consists, as was said earlier, in answering the question of whether on the basis of the biblical idea of God the entirety of reality in which we live reveals itself more comprehensively than on other presuppositions. The Greek conceptions of an eternal cosmic order as transformed into a way of observation of the laws of nature have made an impact on classical physics. In contrast with this view, the possibility of an answer has its basis in the fact that, on the basis of the biblical idea of God, all occurrences were experienced as contingent. The world as a whole, including humanity, was thought of as the contingent divinely established reality: our belief in creation says so. Its problem is in the question of whether the presence of order, the substratum of formulas of law, also can be understood from the contingency of occurrences. Only in this way would it be convincing that the order of the laws of nature on its part also is comprehended by the thought of creation and is not opposed to it. Is the understanding of reality under the sign of contingency of occurrences able to enlighten also that which is seemingly opposed to it, namely, the order of the laws of nature? Here and only here might it be revealed that the understanding of reality based on the biblical idea of God is more comprehensive than the interpretations of the universe proceeding from the Greek view of the entire reality as cosmos, in the sense of a timeless order.[21] At present, this question has hardly been approached, let alone solved. Here also it is possible only to show in some points the direction in which perhaps a solution may be sought. However, first some methodological viewpoints need to be discussed.

It would in any case not be appropriate to the task before us— whether it is solvable or not—to look for its solution in the field of physical argumentation. For natural science questions nature principally by asking how far it satisfies affirmations of laws. But the task before us demands that we view natural regularity itself under an aspect that is different from it, namely, under the aspect of its understandability on the basis of the contingency of occurrences, or from *that* idea of God on the the basis of which the contingency of occurrences has become significant for the understanding of reality as a whole. Such a thought process has to refer indeed to problems and results of physics and other natural sciences but with questioning that is different from that of physics. Therefore it has to have a different structure than a physical thought process, not because of a lack of exactness but exactly for the sake of its appropriateness to its special task. In the theology of nature it cannot be a question of affirming pseudophysical competitive theories. Nevertheless, according to my proposed method, viewpoints should arise that could be of interest also for the investigations of a physicist, not because physical hypotheses or insights can be derived from them but because they open up and enlarge the intellectual space on which the formation of physical hypotheses depend. On this point we can see how modern physics shows traces of its origin in an intellectual context that is influenced by the Christian tradition. The spontaneity of the formulation of hypotheses which only afterward are subjected to especially devised experiments—a procedure we take quite for granted—has perhaps become possible because of the Christian understanding of the place of the human being in the cosmos in the thinking of Nicholas of Cusa. Especially the interest in a history of nature (which will occupy us further) is most likely determined by the biblical Christian thinking in historical terms. In physics also, horizons of questioning have to be opened up first of all in order that hypotheses that arise in them can be examined by experiment and classified theoretically.

The uniqueness of the task of comprehending the regularity of nature itself in the horizon of the contingency of occurrences, as they are viewed on the basis of the biblical idea of God, is especially clear in view of the already mentioned circumstance that the idea of God cannot be founded on physics.[22] The meaning of the word "God" can, since the beginning of modern times, be determined only by anthropology. However, this is more a method for demonstrating the questionableness of human existence than for obtaining knowledge of the reality of God. The questionableness of human existence points in a direction that can be characterized preliminarily by the expression "God." An answer to this questionableness of human existence can be found only in the history of religion; and indeed in each religion in a different and still preliminary way. Only at the question of the viability of the religious answer in the light of the entirety of the experience of reality does the relationship of the idea of God to the knowledge of nature formulated by natural science come into play. The question of the relationship of the idea of God to the knowledge of nature in each case cannot be avoided; for the divinity of a god asserted by a certain religion depends on the circumstance that on its basis the entirety of all that is real reveals itself as a unity. Without presupposing this comprehensive idea of God reality could not be understood as a unity in depth. However, as important as the explanation of this relationship is or as decisive as it is for the idea of God in any religion, it does not serve the derivation of the idea of God but only a successive examination of its significance, of its truth. The idea of God, given by historical tradition, appears here formally as a hypothesis; and the God hypothesis has to prove itself in the wholeness of experience. This viewpoint inserts the process of thinking which is here pursued methodologically into the modern understanding of scientific methodology as such. The methodology of modern science is throughout constituted by the contrast of freely conceived hypotheses or models,[23] on the one hand, and procedures for examining them, on the other hand, procedures that are different in the different disciplines.[24]

Contingency and Continuity

The first preparatory task of a theology of nature was shown to be the discussion of the question of whether the order of occurrences which is describable as regularity can itself be understood as a way of its contingency, that is, as founded on contingent occurrences. An argument pointing in this direction is found in the fact that every relation of the form "if—then" contains in essence a contingent part at its beginning. But we want to attempt to penetrate more deeply into the meaning of such a conditioning of regular connections to contingent beginning links, especially also with reference to the special contingency of time. We resume here once more a theological example: we want to observe whether the understanding of the contingency of occurrences as actions of the biblical God throws light on the conceivability of order and regularity in the horizon of the contingency of occurrences.

Such a connection presents itself in the biblical understanding of reality as history. The structure of this historical understanding of reality is to be sketched first in a few lines before the question is asked whether "nature" can be included in history (broadly conceived) or whether nature represents a special realm comparable to and parallel to history (conceived as human history).

The Israelites understood all of reality as history, that is, as historical actions of their God. This view did not come about at once but step by step and in the measure in which the problem of the "entire reality" as such was faced by the thinking of the Israelites. At first only narrowly limited themes, such as the succession of Solomon to the throne of David, became objects of historical description. Such events were held together by the tension of a preceding divine promise and its fulfillment which finally came about after many intervening events. Already the Yahwist in the tenth century described the entire course of time from God's promises to Abraham to the occupation of Palestine by Israel in the form of such a description of history. The Yahwist even opened with a prehistory going back to the creation of the world before the promise to Abraham. Under the influence of prophecy, this manner of viewing events was broadened to include the future as well as the world of nations beyond the borders of Israel. In the postexilic period, so-called apocalyptic began to understand all occurrences, from the creation of the world to its future end, as a history of the world which is determined by an eternal plan of God and described in symbolic abbreviations. However, in apocalyptic the contingency of historical occurrences was covered up. I presuppose all this background as given and now inquire about the special structure of this understanding of reality. Certain differences between the biblical writings must be left aside here.

1. As the first thing, we must recall once more what was already stressed as the fundamental element of the contingency of occurrences: again and again something new happens, without prece-

dence. And exactly in this, Israel experienced ever anew the power of its God. History presents itself as a series of ever-new occurrences, which despite many similarities are unforeseen. Their course is irreversible.[25]

2. Nevertheless, connections in occurrences arise. However, these connections become visible only from each end of a process. It is important to see what the result of such a matter is. Every event throws new light on earlier occurrences; this now appears in new connections. This fact seems to have possessed considerable weight for the thinking of the Israelites. Their thinking implied, one might say, an eschatological ontology: if only the future will teach what is the significance of an event, then the "essence" of an event or occurrence is never completely finished in the present. Only after the larger connection of occurrences to which an event belongs has been completed can the true essence of the individual event be recognized. In the last analysis, only the ultimate future will decide about its peculiarity. Therefore the idea of an ultimate future belongs to the logic of this view of reality.[26] Here creation itself would have to be considered from its end: on the basis of the final occurrences, God would have designed the world and its course. From this it would result that, at present, creation could be considered only partially by us. It is not yet completed. Only in the eschatological future will we be able to look at creation as a whole and understand it as far as we will participate in the glory of its creator.[27]

The image of a creation that is not completed already at its beginning but whose beginnings are already determined on the basis of the end is capable of making clear the significant consequences that the historical understanding of reality has—namely, only the end shows what is important in an event. I suppose this is more than merely an image.

The fact that events throw light on earlier occurrences and so establish repeatedly in a new way connections backward lays the foundation for the continuity of history. The continuity of occurrences cannot be imagined as a whole as development—in any case, not as development in the strictest sense of an entelechially directed process, that is, not as the unfolding of germlike beginnings. Indeed, there are partial development tendencies within the total process. But they never determine the totality of occurrences. Otherwise there would not be true contingency. Contingency and a purposefulness that directs everything from the beginning (in the sense of entelechy) exclude each other.[28] Only the context which results from each new event backward can be reconciled with the contingency of occurrences. Only by the light that falls backward from present to earlier occurrences can we see continuity without negating thereby uniqueness. Such "continuity backward" is conceivable as a final mode of the connection of all occurrences.

The contingency of occurrences is irreconcilable with a pre-planned purposefulness built into the total process. Contingency is also irreconcilable with a thoroughgoing constancy of forms of process. Constant forms of natural processes are by definition only abstract partial aspects in the contingent process of occurrences. The forms of process by no means have to be "broken through" by that which is "new" in the occurrences. They can be, so to speak, "overformed," be included in a new total context. This happens again and again with the technical use of insights into processes of natural law by human engineers. It also applies perhaps to the process of learning something new about an object in relation to former conceptions of it. Beyond that, the question is raised whether such an "overforming" of that which is given in other ways is a human phenomenon, and as such only a general feature of every relationship of later events to former ones. In this case, that which is ever new in each occurrence would be preserved as such in the strict sense, that is, as not exhausted by the constancy of the forms of process that are already existing.

The historical continuity of contingent events which becomes visible from the end is thus distinguished from the continuity of occurrences described by laws of nature. However, historical continuity can comprise the latter, at least insofar as the appearance of connections by the laws of nature is itself contingent. We will return later to this point.

3. The true phenomenon of historical continuity backward raises the question of the reality which reveals itself in it. Is only the perspective of human beings who experience history expressed in it? Or is here as elsewhere the uniqueness of human experience related to the uniqueness of the reality given prior to it, thus making recognizable something of it?

The fact that events—especially if they are decisive—throw light back on former events is closely connected with the human experience of time. Human beings never live only in the now. Rather, they experience their present as heirs of a past and as its active change. They anticipate the future in fear, hope, and planning; and in the light of such anticipation of the future they return to their present and the heritage of their past. The fact that we know of historical continuity is at least also conditioned by this peculiarity of human experience with time. If there is a new event, then it modifies the context of our consciousness of time which is already *found present*.

It throws light back on earlier occurrences which have become a part of our experience already. In the same way, ideas that occur to us throw light on our previous expectations and plans in justifying, fulfilling, modifying, or disappointing and thwarting them. Thus the contingent event always enters already into a context of experience or tradition. Each event is something that happens to us from the future which is until then still unrealized. It establishes anew the connection with that which happened earlier by altering the context of experience previously found in our historical experience.

Is the human consciousness of time which establishes a context then the only reason that the contingent events throw light for us on earlier occurrences? Or is it a part of the contingent new events themselves that they relate to that which is past? Such questions are deeply intertwined in the problems of the theory of knowing. Yet there is reason for the assumption that our experience does not merely create the unity of experienced occurrences but already pre-supposes it. The continuity which is proper to our consciousness of time could not discover connections in occurrences if they would not befit the earlier occurrences. So, the events happening now have this power to point us to earlier occurrences in order to understand them anew in their light, obviously not by themselves alone but as omens of a future that decides the nature of the past, a future that begins in them and that our consciousness anticipates by becoming aware of them. The future, beginning in the present happenings, is thus the origin of the perspective in which past occurrences are put by every new experience.

In the Israelite understanding of history, it has, in the last analysis, not been the human experience of time and history or the human action in history which constitutes the connection of the occurrences in the world. Rather, this connection is established by God in his acting. This conviction was fashioned in ancient Israel by the fact that the Israelites knew themselves as explicitly directed to the future through divine promises. Therefore the contingent events of Israelite history were experienced as the way in which Yahweh relates to his promises. This was the case even when present events seemed to deviate and agree only approximately with the previous promises. The understanding of the promises themselves became altered through the process of historical experience. Thus Yahweh was experienced as the one who through his faithfulness lays the foundation for the unity of occurrences by coming back from each new action to earlier ones. He does "not forsake the work of [his] hands" (Ps. 138:8). Seen from the end, the faithfulness of God lays the foundation for the connection in the series of occurrences.

The ancient Israelite understanding of history influenced early Christianity also by way of the postexilic eschatological and apocalyptic expectations. But Christianity started out, in distinction from the deterministic perspective of apocalypticism, with a new experience of that which is contingent in divine action. This ancient theological foundation to the understanding of history has remained effective not only in the Christian theology of history; but it remains in the modern West for philosophy of history and historical methodology in general an open question as to whether the unity of history as such can be based on anything else but theology. If we take into account that individual persons and nations and even cycles of culture cannot guarantee unity for history as a whole; if we add that the unity of humanity as a unity of genus remains an unhistorical abstraction; if we add that the historical interweaving of humanity as a whole can at best be the goal but not the driving subject of the process of history; and if we finally take into account that the entirety of history would also have to comprise its still unrealized future, only then do we become conscious of the grave difficulty of any speaking of "the" history.

Jewish thinking could find the unity of all occurrences in the unity of the historically acting God. Christianity later was able to conceive of history itself as a unity because for Christians the end of history has already become a previous event. The perfection of the human being has already taken place with the appearance of the new human being in the incarnation of the Son of God. It may be doubted whether the idea of the unity of history can at all be separated from these theological roots.[29]

In the present context it is not necessary to engage further in this discussion. Instead, we turn to the question of whether the total reality, with inclusion of nature, is to be characterized in the suggested sense as history. This question is sharpened to the further question of whether in nature also the element of connection, of continuity, can be understood, as in the history of humanity, in the contingent occurrences themselves as a continuity "backward."

Entropy, Big Bang, and the History of Nature

Carl F. von Weizsäcker has undertaken the attempt to sketch a "history of nature" (1948). This attempt is very instructive for our investigation, because at the cue word "history" the concern is the significance of contingency for the understanding of reality, in the sense of the question of a foundation for the connection of occurrences *out of* their contingency. We want to see whether and how with the theme of a "history of nature" the contingency of occurrences comes into the view of the natural scientist.

When speaking of history, von Weizsäcker believes that it concerns quite generally the occurrences in time, insofar as they have the character of irrevocable changes. This involves the idea of the irreversibility and unrepeatability of occurrences. At first sight, such unrepeatability does not seem to apply to natural occurrences: the cosmos repeats its courses without ceasing, in the change of the seasons, in the revolving of the stars. Each day the sun rises again. Each spring the trees grow leaves. But von Weizsäcker demonstrates: "Nature's appearance of being without history is an illusion. All depends on the time scale we use. To the mayfly whose life spans one day, [the human being] is without history; to the human being, the forest; to the forest, the stars; but to a being who has learned to contain within his mind the idea of eternity, even the stars are historical."[30] Ten billion years ago, there probably was neither the sun nor any of the stars known to us.

Thus even in nature the processes do not take place in unchangeably equal and principally irreversible rhythms. Here also irrevocable alterations take place, and the process of events is unique because it is not reversible. Now, it is manifest that the conception of a unique course of occurrences stands in an irrevocable tension to the concept of laws of nature. A characteristic of a law of nature is essentially its repeatability. Only the repetition, the occurrence of the same series of events, lays the foundation for the regularity of a process. It appears difficult to think how a unique, unrepeatable process as the process of the world as a whole can be nevertheless a regular process, that is, a process that not only *includes* regularities but would be, *as a whole,* the case of application of a law. Nevertheless, physics knows of a law the general validity of which leads to the conception of the historicity of nature, an irreversible direction of the world process in its entirety. According to the second law of thermodynamics, the law of entropy, heat can never be completely changed into other forms of energy, while, vice versa, kinetic or electrical energy can be changed completely into heat. Von Weizsäcker explains this by the example of a body that is completely brought to a stop. It has changed its whole kinetic energy into heat. But in the opposite direction it can change its heat again into kinetic energy only to a certain limit, namely, to the balance of its temperature with its environment. "The production of heat is to some extent irreversible." The part of heat energy that is no longer able to work, the entropy, can increase or remain the same within a closed system

but cannot decrease. This characterizes the irreversibility of occurrences as it follows from the second law of thermodynamics. Since
every natural process produces heat, von Weizsäcker can conclude
that "every event is in the strict sense irreversible. . . . Hence, no
event in nature is repeated exactly. Nature is a unique course of
events. The final state would be one in which all motion has come to
rest, in which all differences in temperature have been equalized."[31]
This "heat death" can be predicted for the world as a whole, even if
only in the very far future, under the condition that the world as a
whole is a closed system and thus finite, that no new amounts of
energy stream into this closed system or originate spontaneously in
it, and that the validity of the law of entropy is unlimited.

First, the peculiarity has to be pointed out once more that, with the
second law of thermodynamics, a physical law, part of which is unrepeatability, leads through its consequences to the affirmation of the
unrepeatability of processes in nature. Indeed here also, this is derived from repeated observations of individual cases of change from
nonthermal energy into heat. But with the application of the law to
the process of the world as a whole, we pose questions having an
effect backward in regard to the concept of the law of nature itself.

The fruitfulness of the second law for the understanding of a
"history of the cosmos" in the sense of von Weizsäcker comes about
mainly from its statistical formulation. According to this formulation, every condition of energy changes according to thermodynamic probability. Although the macro-state of a body can be
measured for thermodynamic characteristics such as pressure or
temperature or density, the micro-state of its individual atoms cannot be measured directly. The micro-state must be measured indi-
rectly, that is, statistically. No one single micro-state is required to
correspond directly to its macro-state. Thermodynamic probability
provides statistical order at the macro-level to measure the disorder
at the micro-level in the ongoing sequence of thermal events.

Von Weizsäcker connects this sequence with the observation that
the various star systems move farther and farther apart; and they do
that in such a way that the farthest removed ones move away at the
same time with the greatest speed. "The universe we know is expanding."[32] From this, one can draw inversely the conclusion that in
the past the star systems were closer together, and one can figure out
that a few billion years ago the entire material world must have
been condensed in the smallest space. Von Weizsäcker compares the
starting point of the process with the explosion of a grenade the
pieces of which would correspond to the star systems. Those among
them which are on the way close to the speed of light are today

about as many light-years distant from the center of the expanding cosmos as its age has years.

From the original explosion, according to von Weizsäcker, diffuse masses of gas proceeded. These were in turbulent movement. This resulted in differences in weight. These led to the phenomenon that the turbulent movement changed into rotating movement and this led to the formation of solid globes. From the combined effects of turbulence and rotation the individual deviations of the individual systems can be explained statistically so that they contain an element of contingency of occurrences. Thus, von Weizsäcker himself says that the agglomeration of matter of the turbulently moving gases must have been "by accident" denser in one point than in others; then with the attraction of further matter from the surroundings, the transition to rotation took place. The combined effects of turbulence and rotation tendencies at the origin of fields of gravity, which, however, also can be dissolved by turbulence, explain "the regularity in general, and the variety in detail, that are the distinctive features of the spiral nebulae."[33]

The conception of von Weizsäcker is, as he himself emphasizes, not the only possible model of the world process. It only is, as von Weizsäcker points out, the most conservative one among the models possible at present. It is conservative insofar as the unchangeable validity of known laws of nature, in any case some basic laws, is presupposed over large distances in space and time. Furthermore, the design is to be called physically conservative insofar as it relies neither on the addition of new laws of nature nor on the spontaneous origin of new matter in the course of the world process; rather, it presents this as a closed system in the thermodynamic sense. With this is connected the thesis of the finiteness of the world, especially in view of its future.

The "conservative" trait of the design of von Weizsäcker involves two difficulties that in connection with the question of the contingency of occurrences are important for us. The first difficulty is that von Weizsäcker must presuppose a sort of primary miracle, namely, the original explosion or big bang which is supposed to be the starting point of the world process. The question of how this event came about, what perhaps preceded it, cannot be asked in the frame of his design. The difficulty increases when one considers that, if the amount of matter is unchanged, the mass of the universe which several billions of years ago was pressed together in a "narrow space" would have had to squash not only the atom sheaths but also the atomic nuclei. That "narrow space" of the status at the beginning of the design of von Weizsäcker really would have to be a mathematical point.[34] Thus the beginning condition is altogether un-imaginable, and the same is true of the transition to the expansion of the universe. The effort of von Weizsäcker to maintain the amount of matter of the world as constant and the basic laws of nature as unchangeably valid leads to the result, which is worth thinking about, that the beginning of the process contrasts very sharply with the regular naturalness of its continuing process. The naturalness of the process seems to have been purchased with the absolute miracle at the beginning.

Second, the unchangeable validity of the natural laws cannot be unrestrictedly retained in von Weizsäcker's design. Neither the beginning condition nor the transition to the act of that "original explosion" seems to be explicable from the laws of nature. Thus von Weizsäcker himself has raised an objection by asking whether the original event of that cosmic explosion violates the second law of thermodynamics. In starting out from the fact that laws of nature cannot exist ideally as laws *of nature* in themselves in analogy to the Platonic ideas (or merely mathematical formulas), but only in the regularly proceeding material events which are sufficient for them to have their existence, then the judgment can hardly be avoided: in that beginning condition and with that first step of cosmic expansion our laws of nature "were" not yet "in existence."

These remarks are not to be constructed as fundamentally denying the process of extrapolation from physical laws for the purpose of cosmological contemplations. In any other manner, one will hardly be able to reach somehow well-founded conceptions of what nature truly is. But it is true that this way of thinking is connected with peculiar difficulties which were first to be observed with von Weizsäcker's model.

Still a further trait in von Weizsäcker's model of the world process appears noteworthy for our questioning aimed at the relationship between contingency and regularity. At least from an anthropocentric perspective, certain events in the history of nature gain special significance because they make possible the origin of the human race. This chain of natural events seems to furnish the true spine for the development of life because of their linking with each other. The peculiarity of this fact is expressed in von Weizsäcker's question: "The path from clouds to rotary figures and on to spheres is a path from disorder to order, from chaos to form. Is not this contradicting the second law?"[35] Even if this contradiction probably is to be dissolved with von Weizsäcker as only an apparent one,[36] this central episode in the history of nature is probably not exactly what would be expected from an abstract formula of the second law.

Yet after the formation of heavenly bodies came about, the origin of an earth remained the exception from the rule. And again among the events of the history of the earth, the origin of life was also an exception. And something similar applies to the phylogenetic process which leads from the beginning of life on earth to the origin of humanity. This pathway depends on the supposition that among a multitude of spontaneous mutations repeatedly fortuitous exceptions appeared and became the basis of further formation. This astonishing chain of exceptions in which every link furnishes the presupposition for the possibility of the next one makes it understandable that Alfred North Whitehead, as before him Henri Bergson, assumed a "power" in the occurrences of nature which is opposed to the "downward" directed effect of the law of entropy; it is a power directed toward regularity, a power that leads "upward" by way of all kinds of fortuitous exceptions.[37] The assumption of a violation of the law of entropy is here certainly erroneous. But if we permit ourselves to think of the way of nature anthropocentrically as directed toward humanity—and we think of an object never differently than in relation to us as the subject—then the episodes on this pathway seem to be characterized by a sequence of great exceptions; and the technological redirection of nature by the human race makes use of the lee side of the usual, thereby permitting a human home in nature. Yet exactly the significance for humanity which belongs to the reliability of the laws of nature demonstrates that only the mass of the ordinary makes possible the life of the exception. On the other hand and conversely, the extraordinary ideas and discoveries on the road of human history were necessary in order that the occurrences of nature could be claimed more and more in their overwhelming ordinariness and regularity as the basis of human existence.

Historical Nature vs. Steady State Cosmology

The idea of a unique "history of nature" that proceeds in an irreversible process, explained here in the design of von Weizsäcker,[38] has been contrasted with other conceptions. Among these, the steady state model of British mathematician and physicist Hermann Bondi,[39] has become the best-known design and gives the most interesting aspects for the problem of contingency. According to Bondi's conception, it is entirely possible to combine the red shift in the spectrum and the progressive removal of the star systems from each other, which is indicated by it, with a conception of the universe that remains generally the same in each point of time although its individual parts—even stars and galaxies—age. Bondi affirmed a steady state of the universe especially in view of a steady medium density of matter in world space which again makes possible an invariable power of gravitation. In view of the expansion of the existing star systems, this is imaginable only under the condition that new matter originates constantly,[40] being condensed into new stars and galaxies. Such an assumption violates indeed the principle of the preservation of matter. But the violation is quantitatively so small that the validity of the principle remains valid for normal experience.[41] It is only demoted to a formula of approximation.

This is not the place to discuss the empirical truth criteria of this theory.[42] As Bondi himself emphasizes, the special scientific fruitfulness of his theses consists in the formulation of these criteria.[43] However, the question of the intentions that determine the model of Bondi must be asked here. The further question follows of whether the tests, given by Bondi, exhaust the conditions of a falsification of his model.

The guiding interest of the model is clearly pronounced by Bondi: its basis consists in the "assumption that the universe is not only uniform in space, but also unchanging in time when viewed on a sufficiently large scale."[44] Thus Bondi is concerned with the independence of the structures of the universe from time and thus also of the validity of physical laws; for "if we assume that all the physics we know is unchangeable, although the universe is changing, then we make a possible but quite arbitrary assumption."[45] If one wants to maintain the validity of the laws of nature independent from time, then one will have to assume with Bondi that the structures of the universe also are always the same.[46] Yet Bondi is not satisfied with this postulate. He also affirms that the assumption of the uniformity is the most natural and likely one; for all natural science rests on the extrapolation of experiences that—viewed cosmologically—have been gathered by humanity during a rather short period. Natural science has to presuppose the more general applicability of these experiences.[47]

The at least heuristic significance of the extrapolation cannot be controversial. But has Bondi actually developed his model in every aspect by generalization of present experience? This is by no means the case. Experience does not teach that time, or, more exactly, differences of the point in time, are not important. Indeed, classical natural science has abstracted from such differences; and since the formulation of the second law of thermodynamics, the abstract character of the formulas of classical physics independent of time has been recognized more clearly.[48] The interest in such abstract formulas is based on the fact that we human beings want to apply *at a different time* the same knowledge of structure. If the change in time were not important, then the abstract knowledge of the structures would lose its interest. The abstracted structure holds our interest because it permits us to count on an element of identity in that which is not identical. The fact that Bondi affirms without further ado the uniformity in time and space as the property of the universe itself is therefore not based on an extrapolation of present experience but on a misunderstanding of the abstract character of scientific formulas. My observation does not actually refute the cosmological assertions of Bondi's model, but it tends to shake confidence in the basic assumption Bondi values so highly.

In addition, there is the fact that the inference of the irreversibility of all natural events, which results from the second law of thermodynamics, resists the thesis of a steady state of the universe as a whole. It is true that Bondi does not come into conflict with the second law because he does not see the universe as a closed system; he counts on a constantly new origination of matter. But this is now the point where the purely hypothetical character of this assumption has to be stressed, while, on the other hand, the inferences from the second law have the advantage of being based on the generalization of experiential knowledge. Under these circumstances, even a confirmation of the specific cosmological predictions of Bondi would not be able to corroborate the more far-reaching demand of his own model to present the structure of the universe as independent from time. His model cannot stand when confronted with the theories that connect the idea of an irreversible "history" of the universe with the phenomenon of the expansion of the star systems. His model requires proof of a continuing new origination not only of stars and star systems but also of matter. Even should he gain proof, other models are still plausible which describe the cosmos as a unique and irreversible process. The cosmological model developed by Pascual Jordan furnishes an example for this.[49]

It is not for the purpose of achieving a constant medium density of matter in space that Jordan makes use of the idea of a continued new origin of matter. He follows the evolutionary interpretation of the expansion of the universe, which is indicated by the red shift in the spectrum; and he counts, like Lemaître and von Weizsäcker, on the beginning of the process a few billions of years ago. Yet he avoids the paradox of an extreme intensification of the entire present world matter in the beginning state of the world process and thus also the conception of an original explosion by assuming the continued origin of new matter. This idea has for him the function of guaranteeing a greater unity of the various stages of the cosmic process. Jordan assumes further that the new origin of matter stands in an exact proportion to the age of the cosmos, so that the number of protons is constantly approximately equal to the square of its age. In this manner Jordan can assume that in the beginning stage of the cosmos only a single pair of elementary particles, a proton and an electron, was in existence instead of the entire world matter that is in existence today. In the progress of time, constantly new matter comes into existence. Time itself is here thought of as creative, or at least the creative new origin of matter is thought of as a function of time. Jordan bases this conception on the relationship of gravitation and electrical attraction. The latter is 10^{40} times greater than the former. This number agrees in a striking way with today's age of the world, expressed as a multiple of elementary time, that is, of the time that light needs to rush through the diameter of an electron. Therefore, Jordan asserts, following Paul Dirac, that the gravitational attraction between the elementary particles decreases in inverse proportion to the age of the world.

Jordan's model has, on the basis of the scientific ideal of methods, the disadvantage, in comparison with von Weizsäcker's model, that it does not get by without postulating new laws of nature, as von Weizsäcker says. And Jordan must not only affirm new laws of nature but he also must limit principles that so far were valid without exception, such as that of the conservation of matter—just as in the steady state theory.[50] Furthermore, he counts on the alteration of other laws, such as gravitation. However, according to Jordan's model, the alterations of gravitation appear as the function of another law of nature which is more fundamental and on its own part unchangeably valid, namely, of the law of constant relationship between mass and age of the world. The disadvantage of such postulates of new laws of nature and of the alteration of formulas, so far confirmed throughout by experience, appears, however, under a different point of view, as an advantage of Jordan's theory; for if the material world is in a process of a unique and irreversible alteration, then it seems indeed more plausible that the laws of nature operating in it are not valid unchangeably. The laws of nature are not in analogy with the Platonic ideas, existing already prior to the advent of a material world.[51]

A second difficulty of the theory of Jordan appears when one asks how the increase of world matter by leaps, from the first starting point in which only a single pair of elementary particles existed, is to be conceived. Jordan answers this question just as poorly as does

Bondi. However, in favor of Jordan it can be said that his model does not actually require an answer to this question. His intention is only to assert a regular relationship between the age of the world and its mass, not to answer the question of how the new origin of matter which is to be presupposed here is to be explained. In this place in Jordan's theory, as with Bondi, the contingency of occurrences appears which also could not be eliminated in von Weizsäcker's model. In von Weizsäcker's model it was concentrated just on the starting point of the original explosion and then appeared only again in the turbulent movement and in the exceptional character of the origin of forms moving from the star to the human being. In contrast, in Jordan's model the contingency of occurrences is spread evenly over the whole course of the world process so that there is a stronger unity to the total conception.

It has been shown that the question of the finiteness and irreversibility of the cosmos as a whole does not exclude the assumption of a continued new origination of matter. In the same way, inversely, the uniqueness of the world process has been denied, on the basis of an evolutionary interpretation of the cosmic movement of expansion. Denial of uniqueness is based on the argument that this movement of expansion might be a phase in a pulsating movement of the cosmos that alternates periodically with phases of contraction. This oscillation model, however, is a mere speculative possibility. It lacks specific empirical evidence. W. B. Bonnor has attempted to make its nonexistence plausible by suggesting that the intensive heat at the end of a phase of contraction makes all data disappear which in a later time of new expansion and cooling might indicate the former status of the universe.[52] The proposal of such a model that is not at all founded on empirical data is, interestingly, justified alone by the suggestion that in this manner the universe retains an unlimited past and future, without the necessity of taking refuge in assumptions that violate or arbitrarily limit existing laws of nature, such as the continued new origin of matter.[53] Particularly, Bonnor would like to demonstrate that there is no reason for natural science to capitulate to the question of cosmology and, in respect to the time of eight billion years ago, to leave the field to God.[54]

This last position once more throws light on the circumstance that the multitude of models of a scientific cosmology vying with each other is today by no means conditioned only by differences of the empirical starting points. Ideological interests are at stake. Should a theological interest in the finiteness and irreversible historicity of the world also become involved? In any case, the models discussed demonstrate that today obviously only faith in the infinity and equality of structure to the world, independent from time, is able to appear with such cogency that it can be considered in itself already a rather secure basis from which to postulate the conditions of such a world—whether in the form of continued new origination of matter or in the form of an oscillating universe—without empirical evidence or other theoretical reasons except those ideological motives. In contrast, the assumption of the finiteness and historical uniqueness of the world process confronts the prejudice of our era: its relationship with motifs of the Christian understanding of the world, even if distant, can let it appear immediately suspect. Without the weight of its empirical bases it hardly could hold its own in the discussion.

Regularity as a Methodological Limitation

After the discussion of the theme of a history of nature in the context of a scientific cosmology, we now turn to theology which thinks of the world in the context of a history of divine actions. Can the formula of a history of nature, which was developed particularly by von Weizsäcker but which materially also agrees with Jordan's conception and is not even excluded necessarily by Bondi's model, be claimed by theology without further ado as a presentation of the history of the divine action in creation? No. This would not be justified, because all the discussed models treat of the contingent series of events in the history of the cosmos under the aspect of the regularity of this process, not under the aspect of contingency. The contingency of assurances has been sidelined as a marginal problem. This sidelining takes place in von Weizsäcker with view to the beginnings of the cosmos and the uniqueness and irreversibility of its phases of development, as well as in Jordan in the new origins of matter. In Bondi, the aspect of contingency is completely concentrated on this last point. In the oscillation model of Bonnor, contingency is the most repressed, since the question of the condition of the cosmic process at the beginning is pushed back into the infinite. Instead, more strikingly, an element of arbitrary suppositions, not derived from the givenness of experience, appears on the subjective side of the design. The fact that contingency of occurrence appears in various designs in various manners but always only as a marginal problem demonstrates how physics constricts itself by a methodological limitation to view nature only in terms of regularities. However, already the form of regularity—the hypothetical relation "if—then"—is referred to a beginning link that is contingent in relation to it ("if"). Furthermore, the content of statements of law points to contingency in the occurrences of nature in the measure in which it is determined by the irreversibility of time and by a statistical observation of the events. And at least in the second case this points to historicity. Physical thinking points to contingent phenomena from which it abstracts regularities again and again for methodological reasons. The obtrusiveness of events, on the one hand, is the challenge to further research for connections of regularity and, on the other hand, occasions questions that are no longer physical questions because they aim not at connections of regularity but at the significance of regularity as such for the reality of nature which obviously is to be conceived more comprehensively. The question of whether, on the basis of the contingency of occurrences, their connection, especially their regularity itself and thus the unity of nature, can be comprehended is no longer strictly a scientific question.

It is no longer strictly a scientific question as to whether nature can be understood, in the sense of the foundation to the biblical thinking of history, from the contingency of divine actions. The significance of this last question consists, however, in the fact that, in the biblical conception of history, we are dealing with a case where the connection of occurrences is founded on their contingency, that is, where the unity, which appears again and again in physics, the unity of the opposition of contingency and regularity, is taken into view. However, the question of such a unity is indispensable for a philosophical understanding of the reality with which physics deals. It also cannot be a matter of indifference for the self-understanding of the physicist because the physicist's thinking and acting move in the tension between contingency and regularity. In view of contingency which limits recognized regularity, physicists can become freed for further recognition of new connections of regularity.

The theological question as to whether the connection of the events of nature can be understood in the sense of the biblical conception of history on the basis of the contingency of divine actions, therefore, retains a special status relative to the scientific way of thinking. It cannot be reduced by the mere comparison of scientific results. Yet theology necessarily refers to scientific determinations of the relationship between contingency and regularity. Form and content of the connections of regularity discovered in each case also lay open in each case the uniqueness of the contingency of occurrences to which they refer and from which they are distinguished. Theology will have to find in these circumstances the counterinstances and the proofs by which a theology of nature is tied to the reality of nature.

In this sense, in what follows we have to think about the relationship of contingency and belief in creation and, on the other side, about the relationship of contingency and law of nature. Then, finally, we have to think about the question of conceiving nature as history.

Contingency and Belief in Creation

When natural science, in seeking laws and especially the origin of the present world with its forms and laws, comes upon contingent conditions and events, it opens nature up in such a way that the Christian can discover the expression of the creative act of God. In these findings the manner of God's acting specific to the biblical view of a creative God can be recognized. This is not to be understood in such a way that only the contingent but not the regular features of occurrences are connected to the biblical God who creates. Rather, the existence of certain laws and of a regular order as such can be considered, under certain presuppositions that are still to be discussed, as a contingent fact. Those elements of contingency in the occurrences of nature which at first are opposed to it as a correlative regularity are then at the same time the background into which the existence of laws itself has to be incorporated.

Contingency and creativity are not simple equivalents. Not all contingent occurrences are creative. Destruction also can appear as a contingent event. Contingency in the sense of something that is not given as necessary by what already exists is an indispensable element of creative producing. But in view of that which is to be produced, this has essentially the character of creating love. Only love gives permanence to the content of a contingent act. Thus, the relationship of contingency and regularity emerges already from the concept of creativity: only the repetition of a relation of events causes permanence.[55]

In order that the world can be conceived as creation, as an event of continued creative acting by the biblical God, it is not necessary for natural science always to let stand the same elements of the world process as contingent. Such a requirement would prohibit scientific progress and lead to absurdity. It is not constantly determined at which points the contingency of occurrences appears. This changes constantly in the process of research. One must distinguish between the contingency of the initial conditions of a law and the statistical contingency of the exceptions. The contingency of the initial conditions points only mediately to the contingency of occurrences because it is not related to something preceding as contingent; rather, vice versa, it is contingent insofar as it is the basis for a relation of law. The contingency of the initial conditions has the character of contingency of occurrences only under the condition that these initial conditions cannot be conceived as a necessary result of other, more primitive conditions. But the latter also are contingent, and thus, because of the hypothetical structure of all relations of law, a contingent link always remains at the beginning. One can here perhaps speak of a mediated reference to the contingency of occurrences as the material of all relations of law. With statistical contingency, however, there is some latitude for contingency in the sense of an exception within the statement of law. Here it is a matter of contingency of occurrences because it is an event that is not strictly determined by the initial conditions, although, even in a statistical perspective, the uniqueness of such events is disregarded.

The idea of creation presupposes that the world process as a whole as well as in individual events is defined by the contingency of occurrences which uncovers regularity in only partial aspects in each case. Therefore the conception of a world order that has not come into existence but is eternally without change, perhaps in the sense of the ancient cosmos conceived in accordance with the model of the revolution of the stars, is opposed to the idea of creation. The deistic conception, according to which God indeed has brought forth the world but then withdrawn from it, produces a similar negative result, because the perfection of the divine action has effected the existence of a perfect world machine that runs completely by itself. The deist's world which is entirely determined yet, nevertheless, does not rest in itself but comes into existence by a contingent act, makes an assumption that is no longer in conformity with its own system. Therefore it becomes the necessary task of the theory to avoid this assumption. Such a constructed physics avoids the problems that call for a theological answer. Although even a deterministically closed system remains related to contingent beginning conditions, the significance of this is overlooked.

Time and Eternity

An infinity of a world in space and time would not have to be conceived as an unchangeable order; it could also be conceived as incessant change in which nothing solid remains. The relation of such a conception to the faith in creation is difficult to evaluate.

Cardinal Nicholas of Cusa has considered a world that is infinite in time and space—corresponding to the infinity of God—as a world that is especially befitting the perfection of the creator. This idea remains a marginal possibility for the Christian theology of creation. The difference between God and creature does not have to be eliminated. It is not a cogent objection that two actually infinite entities cannot exist together because they both would limit each other and thus would be finite. Furthermore, even a world unlimited in time and space would still not be actually infinite in the strict sense, since it is in a constant process of becoming and vanishing. Such a world should not be called merely potentially infinite but perhaps virtually infinite. And if everything in it could be subject to change, then the new creation described by theological eschatology could under certain circumstances be combined with this conception. If nature would be conceived only as a process of unceasing and irreversible change of various degrees of radicality, then even the eternity of the world could be combined with the eschatological hope for new life.

In the present situation, however, such an infinity of the world is only an empty possibility for thought. As long as the interpretation of the red shift in the spectrum points to an expansion of the universe which in retrospect forces the assumption of a singular beginning in finite time as the most probable interpretation, one can speak of the finiteness of the world in space and time.[56]

Through the modern insight that time and matter belong together, the old problem, already discussed profoundly by Augustine, has become more transparent: the problem of how the temporal beginning of the world is related to time itself. Because of the connection of time and matter, the conclusion becomes invalid that the beginning of the world in time would have been preceded already by a time. Then it becomes meaningless to speak of a world before the origin of the world. However, this means that the act of creation itself also must not be conceived as a temporal act. This suggests to theology a new formulation of the idea of creation: the divine act of creation does not occur in time—rather, it constitutes an eternal act, contemporaneous with all time, that is, with the entire world process. Yet this world process itself has a temporal beginning, because it takes place in time.

In this sentence, I assert that eternity is contemporaneous with all time. With that, the concept of eternity itself is described by statements of time. With a musical parable one might speak of eternity as the sounding together of all time in a sole present. Elsewhere I have developed this concept of eternity from the human experience of time,[57] from the relativity of the distinction of past, present, and future corresponding to the relativity of the directions in space. In view of the relativity of the modes of time to the aspect of the human being experiencing time, this resulted in the assumption that all time, if it could be, so to speak, surveyed from a "place" outside the course of time, would have to appear as contemporaneous. This assumption is confirmed by a unique phenomenon of the human experience of time through the experience of an "expanded" present in which not only the punctiliar now but everything on which a position may be taken still or already is considered as present. The concept of eternity as the sounding together of all time, achieved in this way, is distinguished from the Greek idea of eternity of changeless existence, as founded on Parmenides and Plato. There the idea of eternity is constituted by the contrast to the world of the senses, to time and change. Understood in the sense of the suggestions above, the concept of eternity comprehends all time and everything temporal in itself—a conception of the relationship of time and eternity that goes back to Augustine and is connected to the Israelite understanding of eternity as unlimited duration throughout time.

The worldview of the theory of relativity also can be understood in the sense of a last contemporaneousness of all events that for us are partitioned into a temporal sequence. The four-dimensional continuum of space and time can be represented symbolically—projected on a three-dimensional image—as a cylinder or (under consideration of the progressive expansion of the world) as a cone or sphere. In these images, the entire world process is conceived as a single present. However, it could appear in this manner only from a point of view that would not coincide with any position in the world process.

Eternity so described must not be viewed as the mere sum of that which is scattered in time. Eternity can also be thought of as the production of the content of time which at the same time remains contained in it—in eternity. On this basis the creation of the world would be identical with the creation of the total process of time, and this act could be described as the moment of the independent confronting of the finite moments of the space-time continuum.[58] Thus, creation can be conceived, on the ground of the theory of relativity, as an eternal act that comprises the total process of finite reality, while that which is created, whose existence happens in time, originates and passes away temporally.

It seems that human knowledge, especially scientific knowledge, participates in a certain sense, despite its position in time, in the perspective of eternity. It does so by grasping sequences of events, which occur in time successively, beforehand in their structure of sequence and in their instances. Such participation in eternity, the brokenness of which would have to be discussed more exactly, seems to be confirmed also in the function of knowledge which causes unity. It results through the anticipation of the entirety of the processes occurring in time.

In connection with this, the question arises: What is the relationship of the function of eternity, which comprises all that which is temporal, to the world process itself which takes place in time? Insofar as this is characterized by an increasing unification, eternity enters from the future into time. Of the modes of time, the one closest to the eternal act of creation would not be the past but the future. From the future is the world, even with its already past periods of world process, created.

The understanding of the world as creation, therefore, excludes not only an eternal identical order of the world but also the conception of the world process in the strict sense of a progressive development, of the self-acting unfolding of a germ that was already sowed in the beginning. If natural science should be able to explain the total process of becoming of our world today as development in this strict sense of a teleology closed in on itself, then the idea of creation would become irrelevant. Since such a teleology would exclude any genuine contingency of occurrences within the world process, our knowledge of nature would no longer offer a starting point from which the idea of God—in any case in its biblical form—could become significant for the understanding of nature.[59]

Creation and Differing Cosmological Models

The idea of the world as creation can be explicated in the conception of von Weizsäcker, but also in terms of Jordan's model. So, it becomes evident: the theological doctrine of creation is not bound to this or that individual scientific hypothesis. It can claim different scientific models, although there are conceivable scientific hypotheses which—if they can be verified—would exclude the idea of creation.

If we follow the model of von Weizsäcker, then indeed not the eternal act of creation, which refers to the total process of the cosmos, but its beginning in time would have to be combined with the original explosion at the beginning of the expansion of the universe. The quite inconceivable condition of matter preceding that original explosion should not be confused with the divine origin. This is clear alone by the fact that the act of that original explosion does not become understandable from the preceding condition. A dualism is presupposed here. The act of creation would, rather, be brought into connection with the future of the world, with the line in the history of nature, which runs counter, in the sense of Bergson and Whitehead, to the tendencies of natural regularity left to itself. This line would proceed via turbulent movement to the origin of shapes, further to the origin of life, and finally to the human being. In it, foundational significance for the further course of the history of nature would accrue again and again to the exceptional occurrences.

If we follow the idea of Jordan, then the conception of a creation completed already at the beginning, which successively develops only according to immanent laws, would be more clearly excluded than with von Weizsäcker. Creation is here not completed with the appearance of the first pair of elementary particles in the first moment of time. Rather, new matter originates in each new moment of time. Creation would be thought as occurrences that continue without ceasing. Then the laws themselves or the structures of the occurrences described by them would originate in the world process and would change in its continuation.

It is more difficult to understand the world as creation in the forms of conception of Bondi's steady state model. Here one would have to forgo completely the idea of a temporal beginning; but this would not lead to an unsurmountable difficulty if the idea of creation refers to the entirety of the course of the world rather than merely to its beginning. Bondi's model presents a greater difficulty to theological interpretation by asserting that the contingent new origination of matter "out of nothing," constantly affecting the cosmos, which Bondi himself designates as "continuous creation," is to remain completely irrelevant for the law structure of the cosmos. The hypothesis of a continued new origin of matter has been introduced by Bondi exactly for the purpose of preserving the invariable nature of the shape and order of the universe. One may ask whether it seems plausible, after immensely contingent factors have been admitted in such magnitude, to domesticate this contingency at the same time in such an extreme manner. The acting of God would be limited in this model to the constant care for the necessary supply of new matter for the functioning of the cosmos.

In reference to the first two models of the world process, and with limitation also on the basis of the third, one may speak meaningfully of a creation of the world by God. In all three cases, because of the contingency of occurrences, the difference of God from the world, his transcendence, can be fully affirmed: God distinguishes the world from himself in the fact that God's acting is not conditioned by anything given. Divine acting is therefore accidental, accidental also in the further process of occurrences in relation to that which already exists. The acting of God goes in each case beyond that which is at hand, producing something that is different from it. Divine action is thus finite; and in this way it demonstrates God's difference from the world which came into being by his acting.

In view both of von Weizsäcker and of Jordan and Bondi, one may furthermore speak of continued creative acting by God in the events in the world. With all of them, the origin of shapes appears as an exceptional event in the statistical sense and thereby as contingent. Nevertheless all occurrences happen in such a way that in them what is expressed is that God has bound himself through his contingent acting to certain laws and acts. And God presupposes the material processes that occur in regular forms of succession as the material of further divine acting in which—as will be considered — new forms of processes originate.

Each of the three models sets limits for a theological interpretation at some points. Thus Bondi's model does not exclude the idea of a beginning of the world but robs it of any positive indication. It is more important that one also cannot speak of a historicity of the universe, of a uniqueness in the sequence of its phases of development. Be that as it may, Bondi admits historical uniqueness for each individual system within the universe, particularly for stars and galaxies.

In von Weizsäcker's model, which assumes a temporal beginning of the cosmos, the uniqueness in the sequence of the phases of its history and thus the last uniqueness of each individual event is given. However, a contingent end, which corresponds to the contingent beginning of our world, seems excluded here. The von Weizsäcker model does admit individually exceptional processes, such as the formation of shapes. But in view of the total process one cannot count on such surprises. Only the idea of heat death in a very far future appears as the candidate to end the world. But this picture could be modified by introducing an opposite movement, namely, the power directed "upward" suggested by Bergson and Whitehead. This would carry von Weizsäcker beyond his own statements.

Jordan's model does not exclude a contingent end of our world. Since continuously immense amounts of energy come into existence, the total situation of the universe may very well change fundamentally in a way that is unimaginable for us. Therefore a transformation of our world would be possible, a transformation the depth of which cannot be estimated.

At the basis of some models (von Weizsäcker, Jordan) is the assumption of an irreversibility of the total cosmic process. All refer to the conception of an expanding universe but interpret this phenomenon inconsistently with the sense of a finiteness to the cosmos. If the latter conception would be eliminated, then it would not have to mean a catastrophe for a theology of nature as long as the former remains preserved, whether because of the constant validity of the law of entropy or for other reasons. Even a periodically expanding and contracting universe might be subject to the law of entropy or corresponding factors that give the occurrences an irreversible direction, thereby presupposing that such periodicism would be on its part again only a partial phenomenon within the world process. If the irreversibility of natural occurrences also would be eliminated, then the situation would be much more serious for a theology of nature. Indeed, even then the relativity of all regularity to contingent beginning conditions would remain, as was the case in classical physics. But if the order of nature were conceived as unchangeably constant, then it would push the contingency of the initial conditions and even those of statistical phenomena to the margin. This marginalization of contingency was also characteristic of the worldview of classical physics.

The idea of a world without irreversibility of the sequence of occurrences, however, would have to be judged at present as an empty speculation. All given indications suggest that the conception of the irreversibility of the world process as a whole will stand, even if in the course of nature, directed "downward" by entropy, a contrary factor leading "upward" intervenes.

But the conception of the irreversibility of the world process has backward effects regarding our understanding of the laws of nature. To this we now have to turn more in detail. The following deliberations presuppose the irreversibility of natural occurrences. They do not depend in equal measure on the interpretation of the expanding universe in the sense of a finiteness of the world.

Irreversibility and the Laws of Nature

Our concept of a law of nature is influenced by whether we think of the world as having come into being before finite time, or as engaged in irreversible change, or as an eternally unchangeable order. Under the presupposition of an irreversible process of the world occurrences, even scientifically "conservative" hypotheses, such as that of von Weizsäcker, cannot avoid the question of an origin of the regularities of occurrences in connection with the origin and transformation of the world itself.[60] But if this question is asked, then the laws of nature are taken out of the realm of timeless validity and are put into the comprehensive horizon of a becoming and perhaps also passing world, at least in that of a changing world.

In this connection, I propose the concept of a "continuity on the basis of the end," a bridge building backward, instead of the conception of a forward expanding development. Here we first pay attention to the question of how our knowledge of laws of nature comes into being.

A law in the scientific sense pronounces a constant relationship between two entities or stages, most clearly in the form of the hypothetical formulation "if A, then B." With this it remains open whether A is given. But if A exists, then B also exists. Next to such hypothetical formulations there are also statements of a different structure which state the presuppositions for the formulation of laws. Such laws, however, must be distinguished as principles from the real laws.[61] Only formulations that state the hypothetical relationships of the kind "if A, then B" are to be designated as laws.

In order that the connection between A and B may be discovered, a very simple condition has to be met. The observer must have gone at least once, even if only in imagination, from A to B. In the observer's consciousness, the connection is established only after comprehending B, that is, from the end of the way described by the relation.

Such an observation, however, is not yet sufficient for the establishing of a natural law. One can speak of such only if one can produce B by producing A—that is, in the experiment—or if the prediction "if A, then B" is confirmed repeatedly by observation. The repeatability of the processes is in each case the condition for the discovery of laws. Therefore an occurrence in its uniqueness cannot be comprehended as regular. A unique, not reproducible sequence of A to B does not have a regular character. Indeed, one can treat such a unique event as though it were a case of a possible multitude of similar processes, but that remains pure fiction if one has in reality only a unique occurrence of this kind. Through such a fiction, the process in question does not become a regular one yet. Regularity becomes possible only if several real cases of the same kind are given.

If the world process as a whole represents a unique process that as a whole is unrepeatable, then it also cannot be understood in its entirety as the application of a law. And since each individual occurrence participates in this uniqueness of the total process, since no occurrence is repeated strictly in the same way in which it has taken place earlier, so, strictly speaking, not a single event is expressed exhaustively by the laws that it satitsfies.[62] But how can one in this state of affairs formulate natural laws at all?

The positing of natural laws is possible only if one looks away from the peculiarities that characterize the individuality of each event and that distinguish it from other events of a similar kind and if one focuses on that which is typical, which is common to various occurrences.[63] Everyday experience largely rests on such an abstraction; the fine distinctions of that which is widely similar do not occur to it as long as no special interest urges it upon the observer. Natural law formulates such typical features in the occurrences when it says: a condition of type A is followed by another of type B.

If, on this basis, statements concerning the unique world process are made in such a way that one thinks of the unique total process as a chain of individual events, then the two agree with each other in typical features. That which is unique with conclusions from the red shift in the spectrum or from the second law of thermodynamics consists only in the fact that they lead from all kinds of repeatable processes to a conception of the total process as unrepeatable. Here the execution of the extrapolation goes beyond the scientific question itself which is directed to the connections of regularity.

Let us now return to the statement that the assertion of a regular repeatability of the process "from A to B" already presupposes that the route from A to B at least in thought was taken once and that it could be repeated in the experiment. Perhaps this is the case not only with the *recognition* of connections of law but also in the origin of the forms of process corresponding to them in natural occurrences. As an experiment, this may be considered in what follows.

If natural laws do not exist unchangeably but are related to regularities in the occurrences that originate themselves and change in the process of material reality, then it must have happened at one time for the first time that B followed A. A connection between the two then must have "latched," as it happens according to the opinion of gestalt psychology in the process of perception. Such a latching also has to be considered at the origin of cybernetic regular processes. The latching of the individual sequence from A to B would mean that it tends to reproduce itself constantly: as soon as A appears, B follows.[64]

If this model is correct, then two results follow:

1. The regularities of nature which can be described by natural

laws originate then as *forms of process,* and like all forms they have a certain, but principally limited, stability. They would have the tendency to realize themselves repeatedly without being strictly unchangeable.

2. At the basis of the origin of such a form of process is a sequence from A to B, which is contingent the first time. Furthermore, the connection between A and B would have had to take place at one time for the first time so that the relation A—B has become a form of process. But this connection can have been constituted only when B has happened for the first time, that is, contingently. In this sense, the connection of events between the two is constituted backward from B. This is the way in which the form of process has come about which is then repeated immensely often and therefore describable by natural law—if the supposition is justified that the relationship of natural laws itself is not to be thought of as eternally unchangeable but as originated. The necessity for this follows not only from the assumption, occurring in von Weizsäcker and in Jordan, that the world process has taken its beginning before finite time but also from the fact that experiments to introduce physical methods into theoretical biology have to postulate physical laws that have their realm of applicability only in biology.[65] Such laws, which have their realm of applicability in high molecular structures, as they were not always existing in nature, or only with organisms that did not always exist in nature, obviously were not natural laws before the origin of their realms of applicability but were only mathematical possibilities. If the realm of applicability of a law has come about only in the course of time in nature, then the law itself also as *natural* law is no longer independent of time.

The engaging or latching of certain frequently repeated sequences of events can be produced today in machinery of cybernetic technics also technically, and in such a way that the constructor does not know beforehand what "experiences" his machinery will have. Between the origin of a natural law in the sense of its shape of process and a machine of cybernetic technics, but also of the perception of the shape of a living being, there still remain significant differences. For one, at the origin of shapes of process there is not yet, or at most only in first beginnings, something like a being confronting its environment and reacting to it. The reaction of latching is codetermined at the origin of regular shapes of process at most by other connections in which the events in question take place. Above all, this concerns not the perception of some already given shape but the first origin of shape at all. Before material shapes came into being, there may have been regular shapes of process.

The Contingency of Inertia

The analogy of such latching to inertia also may be worth considering. Inertia as a principle is already at the basis of all laws of nature. If then all shapes of process that can be described by natural laws are to be conceived as originated and subject to time, then inertia also must contain a contingent element. The striving of bodies for remaining in their own condition loses its obviousness on the background of the contingent uniqueness of each natural event. This is significant for the dialogue between natural science and theology, because the principle of inertia has played in Descartes a decisive role for making nature independent toward its divine origin. The principle of inertia removed the philosophical demand for the constant cooperation of a first preserving cause for the preservation of the conditions of bodies and especially also of their movement. However, Descartes still felt the need for a transcendent foundation of inertia itself and saw in it the expression of the unchangeability of the divine creator of nature.[66] In contrast, for later thinkers, inertia appeared as an obvious principle not needing further foundation. If it loses this obviousness in view of the pervading contingency of natural occurrences, then anew the question is raised of the possibility even of this basic shape of uniformity in the occurrences of nature.

Indeed, this question is not raised for scientific theory but for the philosophical reflection on it. In view of the contingency of the origin of uniformity in the unique course of the cosmic process, it can no longer be sufficient to think of inertia with Descartes as an expression of the unchangeability of God. Rather, it can be represented, with other forms of uniformity in natural occurrences, as an expression of God's faithfulness, the identity of which is based not on a natural unchangeability but on adhering to the decisions once made in each case. The question of possibility of uniformity to the laws of nature points beyond all conjectures to be gained from the occurrences in nature. To that extent the faithfulness of God—who, as Israel's experience of God saw it in its history, in all contingency of his acting nevertheless adheres to earlier election and thus manifests in such a way his identity with himself repeatedly—can be asserted as the condition for the fact that forms of process originate at all that can be described by laws of nature. On the basis of the faithfulness of God, by his self-identification in the sequence of his contingent acting, it becomes understandable why the contingent events do not simply accumulate without connection but show the unique inclination to "latch" into solid, regularly repeated forms of process. Only in this way, that continuity of occurrences seems to originate which opens up for us the possibility of numbering arrangements and thus the possibility of formulating regular connections.[67]

Nature and History

The connection of natural occurrences comes into view in the first place by the formulating of natural laws. That is a fact to be contemplated. Natural laws do not describe the unique course of the world process and its partial events. Rather, they formulate certain forms of process that are repeated in typical fashion, forms that appear within the unique total process; and they summarize them. It is remarkable that this access to natural occurrences has been so incomparably more successful than the mythical attempts to comprehend the connection of occurrence in the manner of a narrative sequence. If nature as a whole is in a unique process, then one should think that its events also stand in historical connection, as a narrative sequence represents them which in each case connects unique events to those preceding them. With such a manner of connection, the unique peculiarity of the preceding events, not only their general structure, would be significant for the successive events. In understanding natural occurrences, however, it appears entirely possible to neglect such unique peculiarities and to describe the events as cases of very general rules. Could this mean that the events described by physics refer back less to the individual shape than to certain general elements of structure of the preceding events? That would mean that the process of nature—apart from human beings at first—has not yet gained a corresponding historical continuity in its unique sequence but only a regular one as far as the natural events satisfy process models of equal form. The connection that the extrahuman natural occurrences realize for themselves seems primarily describable by natural laws.

Here an important, perhaps basic, difference between extrahuman natural occurrences and human history must be assumed; for the history of humanity also has, as a unique total process, its continuity at least in a certain sense in itself, namely, through the human consciousness of history which experiences each new event as pointing to the future and in some way to the heritage of the past. Something analogous to this human consciousness of time and its activity which creates connections seems to be missing in the occurrences of extrahuman nature.[68] Indeed, it manifests in the uniqueness of its irreversible process a continuous succession of contingent events, corresponding to human history, but without consciousness of history, therefore also without the ability to represent the connection in this continuous succession. The fact that in the contingent succession of natural occurrences connection nevertheless holds sway is shown by the observation that all higher forms are fashioned from simple forms as their elements. That which is new in each case enters into a connection of regular forms of process which remains intact. It forms it anew, changes it, but never breaches it. Therefore, on the basis of a given system of regularly describable forms of process, occurrences that are contingent in comparison with it must still be considered possible. Thus, new occurrences reveal a new function in that which they find existent. But they reveal this only to us. Extrahuman nature evidently has no ability, comparable to human consciousness, to become aware of the retroactive significance of later events on former ones—aside from "latching" forms of process in the laws of nature.

Certainly one must assume a whole series of in-between stages between natural events on the one hand, whose individuality remains insignificant and which assure the presupposition of further formation only through their massiveness, and the historicity and individuality of the human being on the other hand—which again is shaped only in the process of the history of humanity and is not yet fully realized. Perhaps one may speak of an increasing significance of the individual event and therefore also of a connection of occurrences of a historical kind, connecting unique events, in the transition from inorganic shapes to life and in the process of the development of life. However, it remains valid that the experience of historical connections and thus the consciousness of a history of life as such becomes possible only on the level of human awareness.

But does this justify the denial of the historicity of extrahuman nature in order to reserve history for human consciousness? Would it not be an artificial abstraction to conceive extrahuman nature in itself, separated from the human being, as an entity resting in itself? Does not the human being belong essentially to the wider world process as it is taking place? Indeed, with the inclusion of the human being the state of affairs changes fundamentally. Only with the origin of the human being and with the appropriation of nature by human consciousness does the world process as a whole, retroactively on the basis of the human being, attain its connection in itself. That takes place through human knowledge of nature just as through any alleged dominance over it. Only in this sense is it possible to speak of a history of nature. This is not a history of nature by itself apart from the human being; rather, it is a history of nature directed to the human being. The fact that the connection of the sequence of forms of the world process is demonstrated as a historical connection only from its end, from the human being backward, would correspond only to the manner in which historical connections as such can be constituted, that is, from the end.

The unity of this history of nature can be based indeed just as little, if not less than the unity of the history of humanity, on the human beings themselves. As to the history of humanity, it was shown that its originally religious conception is not as easily accessible to secularization because humanity cannot be seen, as the individual human being can, as the unity-creating subject of occurrences. History receives its unity on the basis of the experience of divine reality as it has been obtained on the Israelite stage of the human history of religions. God makes each new event throw its light on earlier ones and thus creates the historical connection of which the human being becomes aware already before intervening actively in it. It is certainly valid for us human beings to regard our present situation as an already given event in the light of the history of nature, and to do so even if we have to reconstruct the path ourselves. This path has its unity rightfully only under the presupposition of God who has ordained the contingent sequence of forms toward the human being so that this sequence can be conceived as a meaningful connection of occurrences backward, a sequence that is shaped and perfected by human recognizing and acting.

The contemplations of the possibility of natural laws and of contingency and continuity in the process of the origin and shaping of our world today are to be broken off with this prospect. They certainly need more exact examination and more differentiated application and continuation. Preliminarily, much would have been gained with the insight that the themes of theology and the reality that natural sciences describe must not stand side by side without relationship. Rather, it can be possible and meaningful to think of reality as a whole with the inclusion of nature as a process of a history of God with his creatures. The clarification of the idea of God itself, its liberation from features that have called forth justified critique, and its justification in view of the prejudice that speaking of God as such has become invalid, could not be the theme of the deliberations presented here. But at least one motif of the widespread distrust toward the idea of God was demonstrated as groundless: it is incorrect to say that modern knowledge of nature is irreconcilable with faith in God. It is clear that faith in God has to be gained in other areas of life than that of scientific knowledge, but the significance of the idea of God for a connected understanding of nature is just as clear. The connection between the contingency of occurrences and of persevering form, whether of material figures or of regular forms of process, can be interpreted on the basis of the contingency of divine action in the sense of the Israelite-Christian experience of God because God alone remains one and the same in the contingent sequence of all occurrences. The identity of God demonstrates itself in his retaining his former works, as reaching back to that which has already happened on the basis of later events. Such a resumption by God of his former acting gives to human history, just as to the history of nature and its forms, connection and unity. The production of such a connection by a constantly renewed resumption on the basis of what is later to that which is earlier has the stamp of a personal power, not of a mere structure of laws. In this way—and perhaps only in this way—does the unity of occurrences with the preservation of their contingency become understandable.

Notes

1. Because of the usual limitation of the term "creation" to the beginning of the world, one might think of choosing the term "providence" which in tradition designates the divine government of the world as a theological counterterm to that of nature. This is done in the book by W. G. Pollard, *Zufall und Vorsehung* (1960), which is broadly related to the conception of the present study. Yet the concept of providence is so closely related with an understanding of God in the sense of a highest consciousness which has become questionable today that it appears therefore unsuitable. Besides, it always presupposes, in distinction from the concept of creation, the existence of a world that is to be governed by providence and therefore cannot take the place of the concept of creation.
2. This process has been described by John Dillenberger, *Protestant Thought and Natural Science: A Historical Interpretation of the Issues Behind the 500-Year-Old Debate* (New York: Doubleday & Co., 1960), 104–251.
3. It is well known that Karl Barth, *Church Dogmatics,* 4 vols. (Edinburgh: T. & T. Clark, 1936–62), III/1 (1945), has still chosen this way, although he reports in the preface that he considered a different presentation of the doctrine of creation in debate "with the questions of natural science which suggest themselves in this connection" and although he sees here still "rewarding problems" for "future thinkers about the Christian doctrine of creation."
4. The thoughts of Friedrich Gogarten, *Der Mensch zwischen Gott und Welt* (1952), 319ff., go in this direction.
5. The barrier of an only anthropological-existential form of creation faith is not broken through even by G. Altner, *Schöpfungsglaube und*

Entwicklungsgedanke in der protestantischen Theologie zwischen Ernst Haeckel und Teilhard de Chardin (1965), although he turns against the tendency observed in Bultmann, Braun, and Buri that "the nonhuman world is left to itself" (p. 94). Even if one accepts the conception, which was coined by Gogarten despite the polemic of Altner against him (pp. 92f.), that the world "as God's creation is turned over to human beings" (p. 96) and if one agrees with the observation of the harmony between Christian faith and modern natural science (this observation is based on von Weizsäcker (p. 105), in the sense of the freedom of humans toward the world (p. 105), this does not yet involve an answer to the question of whether the God of the Christian faith can be understood as lord of the world, as the reality that determines everything. Or would God be the lord of the world only through mediation of human freedom? Even then it would be presupposed that the world of nature is of such essence that the freedom of humans is not only able to use it but also could proceed from it. In other words, as long as God is to be thought of as creator of freedom—and not perhaps as its creation—he also must be conceivable as creator of nature which contains the conditions for the origin of a free being.

6. This circumstance has to be considered historically just as much as (thus Altner, *Schöpfungsglaube*, 920; cf. 112) the dependence of the rise of modern natural science on the freedom of the human being toward the world which is founded on Christianity. Since only the *emancipation* from the traditional Christian stance which counts on continued interventions of God into the course of events has made natural science possible, the material congruity of both is not to be taken for granted. The vehement debates between theology and natural science that continued for centuries not only were certainly an error but had their reason in the doubtlessly correct impression of theology that modern natural science made the Christian God a God without the world and thus unreal.

7. Karl Heim, *Weltschöpfung und Weltende* (2d ed. 1958). See also the earlier volumes: Karl Heim, *Der christliche Gottesglaube und die Naturwissenschaft* (1949); and idem, *Die Wandlung im naturwissenchaftlichen Weltbild* (1952). On Heim, see H. Timm, *Glaube und Naturwissenschaft in der Theologie Karl Heims* (1968).

8. Already in the second edition of his book *Glaubensgewissheit* (1920), Heim has explained how polar tensions appear in all dimensions of our world experience (pp. 76–132). To this is contrasted, directed by the question of the central view through the whole (p. 134), the category of fate (pp. 173ff.) on which are based the explications of the authority of Christ as "ethical world fate" (pp. 197ff.). On the concept of dimension later: *Glaube und Denken* (1931), 50ff., 164ff., 213f., 307ff. On the concept of the suprapolar: *Weltschöpfung und Weltende*, 76ff.

9. The theological relevance of the concept of contingency has been attacked wrongfully with the statement that contingency is mentioned as a peculiarity of matter in Aristotle. Even if in Marius Victorinus the concept of contingency may be "nothing but a translation of the Aristotelian concept of possibility" (thus G. Picht in his unpublished "Einführung in das Gespräch" for the 11th Göttingen Conversation of Physicists and Theologians of January 28/29, 1961, p. 10, with refer-

ence to Aristotle, *Anal. pr.* 13.32a, 18–20; *Phys.* 235b. 15; *Met.* 1032a 20f.), the concept of possibility has experienced in Christian philosophy and theology of the Middle Ages deep-reaching alterations. This fact is overlooked both by Picht and by Altner who refers to Picht (p. 107). Exactly because the concept of contingency, which in Aristotle lay at the margin of his philosophical interest in the metaphysical world of forms, was combined by Christian theology with the idea of God—something far from the mind of Aristotle—not only a transvaluation but even a deep-reaching new orientation of the concept itself took place (cf. my essay "Akt und Sein im Mittelalter," *Kerygma und Dogma* 7 [1961]: 197–220). This transvaluation and new orientation of the concept of contingency, in comparison with ancient philosophy, has been discussed very insightfully by Hans Blumenberg, *Die Legitimität der Neuzeit* (1966), 113–22, by the comparison of Ockham's doctrine of God with the philosophy of Epicurus.

10. A complex variety of exegetical findings, which may be characterized summarily by the concept of the powerful acting of God, is in harmony with this statement. Cf. E. Wright, *God Who Acts* (London: SCM Press, 1952); and Gerhard von Rad, *Theologie des Alten Testaments* (1957; 5th ed. 1967), 1:112 and passim; Eng. trans.: *Old Testament Theology*, 2 vols. (Edinburgh: Oliver & Boyd; New York: Harper & Row, 1962–65). The concept of contingency lifts out only one aspect of this state of affairs, by preliminary abstraction from its personal character and with limitation to the peculiarity of the occurrences caused by it. Only in this way can the desired common ground for a discussion of the relationship of natural science and theology be found, for divine acting in its personality is not comparable with natural phenomena which may be questioned experimentally. Only insofar as divine acting opens up an aspect in the understanding of events at all does the question of the relationship of theological discourse with natural science, which is occupied with the description of general forms of all events, become discussable. Such a discussion finds its common ground therefore in the interest in events in general and in what constitutes events. The discussion between theology and natural science becomes relevant only when it can be shown that the motif of contingency, which is central for the Jewish/Christian comprehension of events as divine action, opens up an aspect of events that scientific investigation, in any case in the period that was influenced by classical physics, tended to cover up and that, nevertheless, is indispensable as a correlative for the central concept of natural science, regularity, and that has to be considered and is being considered anew in the light of the present broadening of scientific conceptualization. Thus it is clear that the characteristic of reality founded on divine action has its home as contingent already in the horizon of a confrontation of theology with scientific thinking (or, viewed historically, with its predecessor in the shape of the doctrine of nature of Aristotelian scholasticism). If this was done at first in abstraction from the personality of divine action, then the contingency of events could prove to be a point of departure on the basis of which talking about a personality of divine action could become again a meaningful element in the frame of a presently relevant understanding of reality since it is possible that an understanding of reality remains

related in the sign of contingency, in a specific way, at least implicitly, to the conception of God in the Jewish/Christian tradition.

11. Contingency means here (and in what follows) always: that which is not necessary *on the basis of what is past*. In distinction from other contingencies which refer negatively to other concepts of necessity and thus are determined in their particularity—as, e.g., the whole field of physics as applied mathematics is contingent in contrast to pure mathematics—I designate the above-defined contingency as *historical* contingency. It cannot be clarified here what the relation of this contingency is to the specifically quantum theoretical contingency that Süssmann determines by the relationship of that which is measured and that which is not measured. Certainly it does not refer to processes of *measuring*, more likely to each *experience* of history so far, since experience of history belongs essentially to history. Similarities may be assumed in view of the ontological uncertainty (which rests not only on a lack of knowledge and which is not to be restricted to microphysical phenomena but is to be considered at least also for high molecular structures). Similarities also may be assumed in view of a statistical relation to the past, since even historical contingency does not appear completely without relationships.

12. Even Robert Boyle has thought, against Descartes, of the concept of natural law as analogous to positive law; but in modern natural science, Descartes's conception of the unbreakable validity of laws asserted itself. On Boyle, cf. E. A. Burtt, *The Metaphysical Foundations of Modern Physical Science* (New York: Doubleday & Co., 1925; rev. ed., Anchor Books, 1932), 196f. (cited according to the Anchor Book). In any case, Descartes found it still necessary to lay a foundation for the assumption of eternal validity of natural laws, and he named as the foundation for it the unchangeability of God (letter to Mersenne of April 15, 1630, *Oeuvres*, ed. Cousin, 6:108ff.).

13. G. Süssmann called my attention to the essay by O. Chwolson, "Dürfen wir die physikalischen Gesetze auf das Universum anwenden?" in *Scientia*, Rivista di Scienza 8 (1910):42–53. Chwolson explains that the assumption of a homogeneity of the universe cannot be proved even if our astronomical world A (with an assumed diameter of 10,000 light-years) would actually be homogeneous.

14. Günter Ewald therefore states that it is "impossible to give a natural law a definite unalterable form" (*Wirklichkeit, Wissenschaft, Glaube: Die Frage der Wirklichkeit in exakter Wissenschaft und im christlichen Glauben* [Wuppertal, 1963], 18).

15. Thus also Dillenberger, *Protestant Thought*, 284.

16. W. Wiesner, "Christlicher Glaube und modernes Weltbild," *Zeitschrift für systematische Theologie* 3 (1961):367.

17. Ibid.

18. C. F. von Weizsäcker, *Die Geschichte der Natur* (2d ed. 1954), 87; Eng. trans., *The History of Nature* (Chicago: University of Chicago Press, 1949).

19. H. Siedentopf, *Gesetze und Geschichte des Weltalls* (1961), expresses it in such a way that "two different ways of observation, the reduction of natural events to certain mathematical laws on the one hand, and the historical contemplation of natural events on the other hand, are nec-

essary to do justice to the whole colorful fullness of our observations"
(p. 5).

20. C. F. von Weizsäcker, "Kontinuität und Möglichkeit," in *Zum Weltbild der Physik* (6th ed. 1954), 211ff.; quotation on 227.

21. Langdon Gilkey, in his outstanding work, *Maker of Heaven and Earth: A Study of the Christian Doctrine of Creation* (New York: Doubleday & Co., 1959), has seen a philosophical analogy to the physical experiment in the test whether on the basis of certain hypotheses the entirety of experience "seems to become more coherent and intelligible than ever before" (p. 135). Something similar also is, according to Gilkey, to be affirmed for the Christian faith: it "can become the foundation for the most intelligible and coherent understanding of ourselves and the world around us" (p. 138). Basic for this are the "intuitions" "of a dependent, contingent, and yet real finitude and a transcended order" (p. 141 n. 17). See also below, n. 24.

22. The Aristotelianism of Averroës has assigned the proofs for the existence of God to physics, but since physics permits an infinite regress in the series of physical causes, these proofs have lost their cogency. However, in the light of an understanding of reality which is characterized by contingency, it may remain problematic whether the argument that the series of causes of origin, but not that of causes of preservation, may be infinite; because without a first link the effect from which one starts could not exist (Ockham). Even the proof that all finite processes presuppose the activity of a power that is prior to them and cannot be described on their ground, however, would not yet be able to justify the use of the absolutely personal word "God." An interesting demonstration for the fact that the concept of God cannot occur in the methodical horizon of physics is provided by Gilkey, *Maker of Heaven and Earth*, 131: "Scientific method . . . can deal only with variable factors which may or may not be present in an event. It has no way of testing factors which are universally present, for it can set up no experiment that reveals the absence of such a universal factor." This is so because the following is true: "Every fact and event, and every system of facts and events, comes to be in each new moment and is upheld by the active, creative power of God, which continually gives to every creature its power to be in each new moment, and its power to act and relate itself to other creatures" (p. 130).

23. See on this also F. Ferré, *Language, Logic and God* (New York: Harper & Row, 1961), 159ff.

24. On the concept of model and its applicability to natural science and theology, see Günter Ewald, *Naturgesetz und Schöpfung: Zum Verhältnis von Naturwissenschaft und Theologie* (1966), 13ff.

25. See on this my essay "Heilsgeschehen und Geschichte," now in *Grundfragen systematischer Theologie* (1967), 22ff., esp. 23ff.; Eng. trans. by George H. Kehm, *Basic Questions in Theology*, 2 vols. (Philadelphia: Fortress Press, 1970–71), 1:15ff.

26. This element of historical uniqueness also goes beyond the contingency of elementary processes which is considered in quantum physics; for in view of what is unique, even considerations of probability become meaningless. Inversely one may say that even the description of occurrences according to rules of probability still abstracts from their

uniqueness in order to consider them as links in an entirety for the behavior of which certain alternatives are valid which can be expressed by quantitative measures. However, the consideration of several alternatives (in the theory of probability) already signifies a stronger regard to contingency in comparison with the classical theory for which the behavior of a body was determined unambiguously with certain conditions at the beginning (on this, see also Pollard, *Zufall und Vorsehung*, 53f.). The uniqueness that every individual event has in the context of an irreversible history, however, is not yet achieved here.

27. Insofar as this end has become already a reality in Jesus' person and history, theology faces the task to think of Jesus as the mediator of the entire creation, as the divine logos, to whom are all things.

28. Therefore I cannot assent to the statement by Karl Beth, which is so characteristic of the traditional theological apologetics toward modern biology, "that the theory of accident and of the purposelessness of all occurrences directly contradicts the religious world view" *(Der Entwicklungsgedanke und das Christentum*, 33). Also the distinction of development understood as the epigenetic origin of new things, from development as a mere unfolding of preformed structures unfortunately is, for Beth as also for his biological authorities Roux and Driesch, combined with the contrast of a teleological explanation against the mere causal explanation of the phenomena of life; and this has become indefensible today in this form. If Beth, because of his option for a teleological perspective and against accident, contradicted the Darwinian theory of evolution, then the latter, exactly because of the significance that it ascribes to accidents, fits unconstrainedly into the perspective that is developed here.

29. See on this my essay, cited above in n. 25, in *Grundfragen systematischer Theologie* (1967), 36ff., 68ff.; Eng. trans., *Basic Questions*, 1:32ff., 67ff. The attempt of A. Heuss, *Zur Theorie der Weltgeschichte* (1968), shows in an instructive way how difficult it is still today to form a concept of world history without such theological presuppositions. He bases the unity of world history at first on the unity of the human species (pp. 4f.); later he admits the fictive character of such a general concept in view of the historical individuality (pp. 35ff.).

30. Von Weizsäcker, *Geschichte der Natur*, 9f.; Eng. trans., *The History of Nature*, 8.

31. Ibid., 37f.; Eng. trans., 50f.

32. Ibid., 30; Eng. trans., 39.

33. Ibid., 61; Eng. trans., 85.

34. W. B. Bonnor remarks on this point that the "infinite density" of the beginning condition in the model which we met in von Weizsäcker is "a mathematical fiction with no physical meaning" *(Rival Theories of Cosmology: A Symposium and Discussion of Modern Theories of the Structure of the Universe* [London: Oxford University Press, 1960], 7).

35. Von Weizsäcker, *Geschichte der Natur*, 62; Eng. trans., 87.

36. Von Weizsäcker answers to the objection: "The gain in thermodynamic probability of the state brought about by this conversion is so immense that the small loss of probability connected with the formation of regular forms is negligible by comparison" *(Geschichte der Natur*, 63; Eng. trans., 88). With such a large number of events, the appearance even of

rare exceptions is entirely probable in the measure of such rarity, although these exceptions, taken by themselves, remain less and less probable in view of the question whether exactly this or that event will be such an exception.

37. Alfred North Whitehead, *The Function of Reason* (1929; Boston: Beacon Press, 1958), 89; and Henri Bergson, *L'évolution créatrice* (1907; Paris, 1948), 11; cf. 209, 246, 368. The same idea is found also in Pierre Teilhard de Chardin (*Der Mensch im Kosmos*, 2d. ed. [1959], 26), and is constitutive for his concept of radial energy.

38. The model of von Weizsäcker belongs in a group of evolutive interpretations of the cosmos among which especially that of Abbé Lemaître is to be stressed. It also makes the universe pass from a status of extreme density of world matter by a sort of explosion into its movement of expansion. Since with increasing expansion gravity decreases, the gaseous beginning status of matter was able to pass over into a solid state and to the formation of solid bodies.

39. Hermann Bondi, *Cosmology* (Cambridge: Cambridge University Press, 1952). Bondi has furnished a generally understandable explanation of his thoughts in his book *The Universe at Large* (New York: Doubleday & Co., Anchor Books, 1960). A summarizing sketch, authored by Bondi himself, is found also in Bonnor, *Rival Theories*, 12–21.

40. "If we wish to remain true to our assumption (namely that the universe as a whole is invariable), therefore, we have no choice but to postulate that there is going on a continual creation of matter, the appearance of atoms of hydrogen out of nothing" (Bondi, *The Universe at Large*, 42).

41. The rate of "continual creation" of new matter "is far below anything that could be measured directly and does not contradict the experiments or the experiences on which the usual law of conservation of matter is based" (Bondi, *The Universe at Large*, 42f.).

42. The most important of these criteria or tests are, according to Bondi: (1) The structure of the star systems would have to be independent from their distance from us; (2) the number of the very distant systems would have to be smaller than the evolutive theories assume; (3) new systems would have to come into existence constantly; and (4) the origin of more complicated chemical elements has to be possible also under present conditions—e.g., in supernovae and red giants (Bondi, *The Universe at Large*, 47–55).

43. Ibid., 35, 47, and esp. 20.

44. Ibid., 42., Cf. Bonnor, *Rival Theories*, 19: "On the basis of the steady-state theory, time does not matter."

45. Bonnor, *Rival Theories*, 13.

46. Ibid., 16.

47. Bondi, *The Universe at Large*, 42: "For all our science has been learned in—cosmologically speaking—a minute region in a very short period of time. Unless ours is a typical place and time, we cannot have much confidence in the applicability of our science elsewhere in the universe and at other times." Less convincing is the continuation of this sentence that the trust in the possibility of such extrapolation only makes it possible to make "more and better" predictions which are accessible to the test of observation. Such predictions, however, are merely a matter of conclusions from a given model and are thus connected with

its logical implications which remain independent of the amount of trust one puts in such a model.

48. Thus Erhard Scheibe in his book *Die kontingenten Aussagen in der Physik: Axiomatische Untersuchungen zur Ontologie der klassischen Physik und der Quantentheorie* (1964), 52ff., has denied the immediately *ontic* significance of the formulas of classical physics and has reduced them to a primarily "epistemic" sense, i.e., to their function within the classical theory. The relation to reality of this function as a whole is, however, by no means immediately unambiguous but is mediated by the abstraction from the contingent character of occurrences.

49. Pascual Jordan, *Das Bild der modernen Physik* (1948), 113ff. The following quotes in the text refer to this work.

50. Bonnor, in *Rival Theories*, 10f.

51. Thus, one must agree with Bondi that it would be "a possible but quite arbitrary assumption" to count on the unchangeability of physical knowledge of laws when the universe itself is changing (Bonnor, *Rival Theories*, 13). The example of Jordan conveys a distant idea that one can draw from the assertion of Bondi also the opposite consequence, namely, to count seriously with an alteration of the regularities to which formulations of physical laws refer and to change the concept of natural law correspondingly.

52. Bonnor, in *Rival Theories*, 8.

53. Ibid., 11.

54. Ibid., 10, "downing tools and handing over to God 8.000 million years ago."

55. Cf. Alfred North Whitehead, *Science and the Modern World* (1925; New York: New American Library, 1960), 116: endurance is the repetition of the pattern in successive events.

56. On the problem of the infinity of the world, see the essay under this title by C. F. von Weizsäcker in his volume of essays, *Zum Weltbild der Physik* (6th ed. 1954), 118–57.

57. Wolfhart Pannenberg *Was ist der Mensch?* (1962), 50ff.; Eng. trans., Duane A. Priebe, *What Is Man?* (Philadelphia: Fortress Press, 1962), ch. 6.

58. Whitehead, *Science and the Modern World*, 111, thinks that only by the solidification of a structure of occurrences as the effect of a regularity can space and time be differentiated for that which comes into being: it is in this endurance of pattern that time differentiated itself from space.

59. However, this applies only to the immanent teleology of closed developmental processes. The transcendent teleology of the belief in providence which sees the aims of occurrences founded in the transcendency of a divine will governing the course of the world would be quite congruent with contingency on the level of finite events. Scholasticism based on Aristotle has combined both teleologies through the assumption that purposeful processes in nature presuppose an intelligent, aim-setting cause. Exactly this argumentation, however, does not seem to find room in modern conceptions of teleology of natural occurrences which are based on cybernetic forms of self-governing of material processes. Thereby the innerworldly teleology loses its old function of a support for religion and changes into the

most closed model of a process running out of itself for the understanding of which no religious reference is needed. The fact that partial systems of this kind represent exactly the structure of life and—in the highest development—that of human life may, in theological reasoning, appear characteristic both of the independence and freedom into which everything alive and especially the human being is dismissed and for the temptation of the sinful making oneself independent against the divine origin of all life, which is connected with it.

60. Spoken more accurately: the relationship of natural laws within the occurrences of nature itself appears as changeable, i.e., the forms of occurrences described by formulas of law. The mathematical formula of a natural law may have a timeless structure *for itself*. It is a *law of nature* only if it refers to contingent data and describes their structure of order, their form of process, which, however, on its part cannot be one that can be repeated at any time in a strictly identical manner if the world process as a whole occurs uniquely and irreversibly. Then the regularities of nature can be treated only in such a way *as if* they were strictly identical, and for most practical purposes the inexactness that is caused by it may be neglected.

61. On this difference, see J. König, "Bemerkungen über den Begriff der Ursache," in *Das Problem der Gesetzlichkeit* (1949), 1:25ff.

62. Let us remember once more the thesis of von Weizsäcker of the "inexhaustibility of the real by individual recognition of structure" ("Kontinuität und Möglichkeit," in *Zum Weltbild der Physik*, 227).

63. This is emphasized also by W. Döring, "Naturwissenschaftliche und historische Weltbetrachtung," *Universitas* 14 (1959): 971–80: "Even if we stipulate it as self-understood that nature in principle is ruled by a regularity without exception, i.e., that under identical presuppositions constantly the same event occurs, we can doubt the exceptionless validity of the discovered natural laws because all conditions for two processes are in reality never exactly identical. Only for those phenomena for which existing differences play no role, can natural laws be established. But for an event in which the presuppositions essential for its process were realized only once and can never be reproduced, there are no natural laws" (p. 974). Because the agreement of processes in natural occurrences is everywhere only partial, one cannot distinguish strictly between physical and historically unique *processes* but only between the related ways of observation, "depending on whether one pays attention to the repeatable or unique features" (p. 978). I owe the reference to this article to Prof. A. M. K. Müller, Braunschweig.

64. Already Hume has recognized in his critique of the concept of causality that A does not actually produce B but rather that only a constantly recurring, solid relation exists between the two. Cf. also König above at n. 61.

65. See on this Walter M. Elsasser, *The Physical Foundation of Biology* (London and New York: Pergamon Press, 1958); and idem, "Max Borns Kritik der mechanischen Vorhersagbarkeit und die theoretische Biologie," in the *Festschrift zum 80. Geburtstag von Max Born* (1963).

66. Descartes, *Principia philosophiae* II, 37; cf. above, n. 12.

67. Von Weizsäcker, "Kontinuität und Möglichkeit," 223: "The continuity of what is real is expressed for us as the possibility of arranging."

68. The *consciousness* of history most likely is more difficult to separate from occurrences of history than it appears in von Weizsäcker, who says very apropos of nature, "Nature undergoes history, but she does not experience it. She is history but does not have history, because she does not know that she is history" (*Geschichte der Natur,* 11; Eng. trans., 9). This might also be said apropos of the human race.

5

The Doctrine of the Spirit
and the Task
of a Theology of Nature

When the second ecumenical council at Constantinople in 381 complemented the Creed of Nicaea, the first of the additions to its third article was to call the Holy Spirit the one who gives life (*pneuma zōopoioun*). This language, of course, was no innovation but was reminiscent of the way the New Testament writings had spoken of the Spirit. Especially Paul and John had called the Spirit the quickening one, the one who gives life. Today this is often interpreted in a restrictive way as a purely soteriological expression referring to the new life of faith, and certainly this is in the focus of the early Christian writings. But the phrase is by no means to be restricted to the life of faith. There are a number of words that in mentioning the life-giving spirit explicitly refer to the resurrection of the dead. And at least Paul alludes to the breath of life (*pnoē zōēs*) that, according to Gen. 2:7, was given to the first man, when he says in 1 Cor. 15:45 that while the first man was created a living soul, the last man will be life-giving spirit. That Adam was created a living soul is an explicit quotation from Gen. 2:7. There it is presented as an effect of the breath of life being inspired by God into man's nose. This breath of life (*pnoē zōēs*) was taken by Philo of Alexandria as spirit of life (*pneuma zōēs*), and in a similar way Paul's assertion that the second Adam will be life-giving spirit and not only a living soul refers to the breath of life that God inspired into the human body when he created the human race. Thus, if we want to understand Paul's idea of the new humanity, we have first to explore the Old Testament background of his statement. It is precisely the idea of the spirit as the origin of all life.

This idea was very common in the ancient world. It was considered an empirical fact that with the last breath life is leaving the body. Hence the mysterious power of life was widely understood to be identical with breath. Therefore the soul as the power of life, and breath and spirit, were closely related not only in the ancient Near East, but also in Greek thought. The terms *pneuma* and *pnoē* or breath were associated, and by *pneuma* nothing else was meant than the air we breathe. This explains how one of the earliest Greek philosophers, Anaximenes from Miletus, came to consider the air as the origin of all things. It was on this line that later on Anaxagoras proclaimed the mind as the ruler of the cosmos, the difference being mainly that Anaximenes had considered the human soul an example of the air that pervades everything, while Anaxagoras took it the other way round and conceived of the power pervading the cosmos by analogy with the highest ability of the human soul.

The relation between breath and air permits a closer understanding of the fact that in the Old Testament the divine spirit was closely associated with wind and storm. Thus in the very beginning of the creation, according to Genesis 1, the spirit of God stirred up the waters of the primeval ocean. And the prophet Ezekiel in his great vision of his people's dry and dead bones on the plain saw the spirit of God breathing into the bones after they had taken on flesh and bringing them to life again.

The most pathetic description of the creative function of the divine spirit with regard to life has been given in Psalm 104. The psalm speaks to God of his creatures: "When you hide your face, they are dismayed; when you take away their breath, they die and return to their dust. When you send forth your spirit, they are created; and you renew the face of the ground." The last phrase identifies the divine spirit with those prolific winds which renew the surface of the ground in springtime. Yahweh's spirit had taken over this function from Baal who was a god of storm as well as of fertility.

The life-giving activity of the divine spirit determines the horizon for all other functions that the Old Testament attributes to the spirit of God. There is especially the charismatic element. Not only for prophetic vision and inspiration but also for the work of the artist, for poets and heroes, a special endowment with the spirit of God was considered necessary. These charismatic phenomena, however, were taken to refer to the same power that inspires and animates all life. The charismatic phenomena present just outstanding examples of life. They exhibit a particularly intensified life and are therefore attributed to an exceptional share in the life-giving spirit.

In a similar way Paul's idea of the new life of the resurrection is based on the traditional understanding of life as originating from the creative power of the spirit. The ordinary life is not life in the full sense of the word, because it is perishable. The living beings have only a limited share in the power of life, for according to Gen. 6:3 God has decided that his spirit should not continue to be active in humanity indefinitely, for, after all, we humans are only flesh. Therefore the time of life is limited. When we expire, "the dust returns to the earth as it was, and the spirit returns to God who gave it," says Ecclesiastes (12:7). This, of course, does not imply any immortality of the human soul, but rather its dissolution into the divine spirit of whom it came. Paul discovered an indication for the limited character of the present life in the Genesis report itself, since it speaks only of a living being or soul springing from the creative breath of life. This meant to Paul that the living being is different from the spirit itself, and this fact accounts for the perishable character of our lives. Since our life in form of a soul or a living being is separated from its origin in the creative spirit of God, it has fallen to death. Therefore the question can arise for another life, a true life that persists in communication with its spiritual source. Precisely this comes to expression in Paul's idea of the resurrection life that will be one with the life-giving spirit and therefore immortal. Again, this was not a completely strange idea within the stream of Jewish tradition. Had not the prophets announced a time when the spirit of God will remain on his people and even be poured out on all flesh? The precise meaning of this is nothing less than immortal life, and therefore the resurrection of Christ and the spread of the proclamation of it could be taken as the beginning of the fulfillment of the old promises. In the New Testament the spirit is closely connected with the resurrected Lord, and the presence of the spirit in the Christian community should not be severed from the ongoing proclamation of the resurrection of Christ and from the participation in it by faith and hope. Thus, although the emphasis of the New Testament writings concerning the spirit is on the new life of faith communicated by the spirit and on the spirit's charismatic presence, the deep meaning of those affirmations and their particular logic and rationality is accessible only if one takes into account the basic convictions of the Jewish tradition concerning the spirit as the creative origin of all life.

The Spirit in Creation and Salvation

In Greek patristic theology, as in the Eastern Orthodox tradition until the present time, there has always been preserved a continuous awareness of the fundamental importance of the spirit's participation in the act of creation as providing the basis for the significance of the spirit's soteriological presence in the church and in Christian experience. Certainly, a characteristic intellectualization took place, since the spirit was identified with the wisdom of God. Thus Irenaeus, in order to confirm his assertion that the spirit was already present and active in the creation of the world, appealed to Prov. 3:19: "The LORD by wisdom founded the earth; by understanding he established the heavens; by his spirit the deeps broke forth, and the clouds drop down the dew." He also referred to the myth of wisdom in Proverbs 8 and concluded that the one God has made and ordered everything through his word and his wisdom. But in spite of the intellectualistic overtones of the wisdom tradition, Irenaeus related the spirit especially to the prophetic inspirational experiences and regarded them as a specific example for the more general fact that the spirit of God "from the very beginning" assisted people in adjusting themselves to the actions of God by announcing the future, reporting the past, and interpreting the present. Thus the spirit, according to Irenaeus, was the first to reveal God to humanity. Afterward the Son adopted us and only in the eschaton God will be known as Father in the kingdom of heaven.

Although since the third century the soteriological function of the spirit as a special divine assistance toward the ethical destiny of the human race attracted more and more attention, particularly with the rise of the monastic movement, Athanasius and after him Basil of Caesarea very strongly emphasized the collaboration of the spirit in the work of creation in order to assure the spirit's full divinity. In the Latin church this aspect was hardly ever treated with comparable seriousness. The activity of the Holy Spirit was seen in connection with charity and grace rather than with the creation of life, and the period of the Spirit in the history of salvation was no longer identified with the period of the preparation of humanity for the arrival of the Son of God but rather with the period of the church after the incarnation and after Pentecost. Thus it is not surprising that, with regard to the Reformers, Regin Prenter and other authors have spoken of a rediscovery of the doctrine of the Spirit. Of course the Spirit had never been altogether forgotten in Christian theology. But in medieval theology even in the doctrine of grace the Spirit receded into the background of the idea of a created grace that was considered the supernatural gift communicated through the sacraments. The Reformers, however, because of their biblicism rediscovered and reappropriated for their theology the broad application of the idea of the Spirit in the biblical writings. In this connection, Luther as well as Calvin strongly emphasized the role of the Spirit in the creation, but neither of them developed in a systematic way the consequences for an understanding of nature. This fact explains in part why Protestant theology afterward fell back to a predominantly soteriological conception of the work of the Spirit. This is particularly true of pietism. In the beginning of the seventeenth century Johann Arndt was silent concerning the contribution of the Spirit to the work of creation, Jean de Labadie explicitly denied it, and later on Philipp Jacob Spener mentioned it but treated it like a piece of dead tradition. Thus the Spirit became a factor in subjective experience rather than a principle in explanation of nature. The Cartesian dualism of spirit and matter certainly contributed to the pervading and lasting influence of this subjective interpretation of the doctrine of the spirit.

This subjectivistic bias was further enhanced by the influence of the spiritualistic movement of the sixteenth and seventeenth centuries which developed from medieval mysticism. In this tradition, which also influenced pietism, the Spirit was related to anthropology although not to the world of nature. The Spirit was conceived in correspondence to the inner light in the human mind. This paved the way for the identification of spirit and mind in the idealist tradition under the impact of Cartesian dualism. Even John Locke conceived of the spirit in terms of a substance acting in the operations of the mind, and because David Hume eliminated the idea of substance, he could abolish the idea of spirit altogether. The idealist thinkers, on the other hand, and especially Hegel, developed a new perspective of the universe as created by the Spirit. But they did so on the basis of the Cartesian dualism and of the identification of spirit with mind. Precisely this point proved fatal for idealism, because spirit as absolute mind was shown to be an absolutizing self-projection of the human mind. Thus the identification of spirit and mind became an important argument for the atheism of Ludwig Feuerbach and his famous followers. Christian theology, on the other hand, argued against idealism because of the identification of the divine spirit with the human spirit. This resulted in separating the spirit from the human mind. But then theological talk about the divine spirit lost its last empirical correlate, and consequently it has become almost meaningless. The only function left to it is that of a pretended legitimation for the acceptance of otherwise unintelligible statements of faith. Such an explanation of the work of the spirit is far from overcoming the subjectivism that has been so characteristic of Christian piety in modern times. On the contrary, it represents the peak of that subjectivism, a subjectivism of an irrational decision of faith.

It should be obvious that the appeal to a principle beyond understanding in order to render acceptable what otherwise remains unintelligible does not provide an adequate basis for a responsible doctrine of the Holy Spirit in theology. Nor can we build such a doctrine on the identification of spirit with mind after that has come under so serious and pertinent criticism in the history of modern thought. Nor is it advisable to start again with the reality allegedly disclosed in religious experience, particularly in the experience of "spiritual" regeneration, for that would end up again in the deadlock of subjectivism. In order to find a fresh starting-point in the tradition, we have to go back behind the entire subjectivistic thrust in the history of the doctrine, even behind the isolation of the soteriological concern in dealing with the spirit. Only an understanding of the spirit on the basis of his function in creation and in this regard to his contribution to an explanation of nature can overcome the subjectivistic bias of traditional Christian piety and thought in dealing with the spirit. But can we in any intellectually serious way attribute a function in the explanation of nature to the Holy Spirit?

Beyond Spiritual Subjectivism: Tillich and Teilhard

In modern Christian thought, there are two outstanding examples of an attempt to break through the spiritual subjectivism and to develop a conception of the spirit within the broad horizon of an overall interpretation of life. One is the section on life and the spirit in Paul Tillich's *Systematic Theology*. The other one is the vision developed by Pierre Teilhard de Chardin of the evolutionary process of life as being directed by a spiritual power.

For Tillich, spirit is one of the "dimensions of life" beside the inorganic, the organic, and the psychological dimension. They are potentially present in every living being. Among them, spirit is the "power of animation" and therefore distinct from the different parts of the organic system. Spirit is not identical with mind, although on the level of human life the self-awareness of the animal is taken up into the personal-communal dimension which Tillich calls spirit. Thus the human being is that organism in which the dimension of spirit has become dominant. On the other hand, even the human spirit cannot overcome the ambiguities of life in its constitutive functions of self-integration, self-creation, and self-transcendence. In order to cope with these ambiguities, the divine spirit must assist the human spirit. Tillich thus distinguishes between divine Spirit and human spirit. Only by ecstatic acts the human spirit participates in the divine spirit, and only in this way can we approach the integration and unity of the three regions of spiritual life: culture, morality, and religion.

Tillich himself observed a close similarity of his perspective to Teilhard de Chardin, whose book about "the phenomenon of man" he read after the completion of his own work. There exists indeed a basic similarity in the idea that spirit is the animating power of all life and not identical with mind, although in the emergence of the human consciousness it realizes itself in a decisively new and intensified form. Teilhard and Tillich also agree in emphasizing the tendency of self-transcendence in life, which was called radial energy by Teilhard, while in Tillich's view it relates the human spirit to the divine spirit.

There are also differences, however, between the two approaches. First, Teilhard does not distinguish in the same way as Tillich does between the divine spirit and spirit as a dimension of life. In Teilhard's perspective, there is only one spirit permeating and activating all the material processes and urging them beyond themselves in a process of progressive spiritualization and of converging unification toward a center of perfect unity that in providing the end of the evolutionary process proves to be its true dynamic origin. In such a perspective, created spirit can be only a participation in the dynamics of the one spirit that animates the entire process of evolution. The difference between God and humanity is preserved also in such a perspective, because only in transcending itself a material being participates in the spiritual dynamic. This corresponds to Tillich's emphasis on the self-transcendence of life and on the element of ecstasy in spiritual experience. Tillich presumably retained the dualism of human spirit and divine Spirit because of his method of correlation between question and answer. In reality, however, even within his conception it is difficult to see why the ecstatic element is attributed specifically to the "spiritual presence" of God in faith, hope, and love and not universally to all spiritual experience as exemplifying the self-transcendence of life.

A second difference is that Teilhard does not use the vague and confusing language of "dimensions of life"—a language that at best has metaphorical value in exposing the "one-dimensional" narrow-mindedness of a purely materialistic description of organic life. The weakness of such metaphorical talk about "dimensions of life" consists in the fact that there is, of course, no coordinate system of the dimensions of inorganic, psychological, and spiritual reality. The same interest in the depth of the phenomenon of life that escapes a purely materialistic description is expressed by Teilhard in a much simpler way, when Teilhard spoke of a spiritual inside of every material phenomenon. He shared this view with the old tradition of philosophical animism. But he also offered a justification for it, first by appealing to the principle that scientific exploration should look for the universal rule behind an apparently extraordinary phenomenon as the emergence of the human mind is, and second by maintaining a regular correspondence between the degree of complexity of a physical phenomenon and the level of its interior spirituality. Teilhard's boldest assertion, however, consists in his combination of the spiritual inside of natural phenomena with the energy behind the natural processes.

In the final analysis, Teilhard supposed, all energy is spiritual in character. But since energy manifests itself for physical observation in the interrelations of physical phenomena, Teilhard introduced his famous distinction between a tangential energy or force that accounts for all sorts of "solidarity" of the bodily elements and their interrelations, and a radial energy that explains the self-transcendence of existing phenomena toward increasing complexity and unity. This distinction is due, as I mentioned before, to the basic assertion of the spiritual character of energy. The natural scientists, especially the physicists, concern themselves—as Teilhard explicitly affirmed—only with the exterior manifestation of the cosmic energy in the interrelations of bodies. But if energy, as Teilhard assumes, is essentially spiritual, then there must be another aspect of energy, and this is to be found in the dynamics of self-transcendence which Teilhard calls radial energy.

The problems inherent in this idea become particularly apparent if one asks for aspects of the concept of energy that have not been taken into consideration in Teilhard's thought. Here, the phenomenon of an energetic field deserves particular attention. Classical mechanics dealt with bodies, with their positions in space and time, and with the forces effective in their interrelations. These forces were attributed to the bodies that were understood to exercise a force. But when physical science attempted to reduce the notion of a natural force to a property of the body, especially to its mass, that did not work. For the last time Einstein started on such an attempt. But his theory of relativity ended up with the contrary result. Instead of reducing space to a property of bodies and of their interrelations, it in fact resulted in a conception of matter as a function of space. This marks the definitive turning point from a conception of natural force on the basis of the model of the moving body to an autonomous idea of energy conceived of as a field. The attribution of natural forces to a field of energy as, for example, in the case of an electric or magnetic field means to conceive of energy as the primary reality that transcends the body through which it may manifest itself—a reality that we no longer need to attribute to a body as its subject.

Teilhard de Chardin did not yet fully appreciate this radical change of the concept of natural force from a property of bodies to an independent reality that only manifests itself in the genesis and movements of bodies. To be sure, Teilhard recognized the idea of energy as the most fundamental idea of physics. But he expressed reservations concerning Einstein's field theory. He insisted on the connection of energy to the body, and he expressed this connection by conceiving of energy as a sort of soul even in inorganic bodies.

In the treatment of Teilhard's idea of spirit, the lengthy discussion of the problems connected with the concept of energy may have seemed at first a deviation. Now it becomes apparent that Teilhard's decision for not conceiving energy in terms of a field but in terms of the inside reality—the "Within"—of bodies, has had far-reaching consequences for his understanding of the spirit. In fact, in a certain way it counteracted his basic emphasis on the spirit as a transcendent principle, transcending every given reality but activating it in the direction of a creative unification. If Teilhard had conceived of energy in terms of a field, this would have been in perfect concordance with his idea of a transcendent spirit whose creative power dominates the entire process of evolution. Since, however, he identified energy as the inside reality of bodies, he attributed energy to those bodies. Therefore, even the movement of self-transcendence and thus the entire dynamic of evolution was attributed to finite bodies rather than—as Teilhard wanted to do—to a principle transcending them as it is the case with his point Omega. Thus the basic ambiguity of Teilhard's thought comes to the fore, the ambiguity of what finally sets in motion the evolutionary process: point Omega or the evolving entities themselves. On the basis that energy is attributed to the bodies, the process and the direction of evolution seem to be produced by the evolving species which seem to act like subjects of their own evolution. In this perspective, point Omega appears to be a mere extrapolation of tendencies inherent in the evolutionary process or, more precisely, in the evolving animals themselves. On the other hand, Teilhard wants to explain Omega, the goal of the process of evolution, as being its true creative origin. This he did by describing evolution as the work of a unified spirit who transcends the individual entities and is finally identical with God Omega who creatively and progressively unifies his world.

But Teilhard failed to relate this view adequately to his idea of energy, although spirit and energy designate the same reality in his thought. He conceived of energy only as inside bodies instead of a field transcending the bodies and prior to them. If he had done so, Teilhard could have developed his basic intuition of the world as a process of creative unification by a spiritual dynamic in a more consistent and more convincing way. He need not even surrender the concept of a spiritual inside of bodily phenomena. He had only to add that this is the aspect of the universal field of energy from the finite point of view of the entities through which it manifests itself. They participate in the universal field of energy only by transcending themselves, or by way of ecstasy, and the degree of their capability for that ecstatic experience would mark the degree of their spirituality. Thus, Paul Tillich's idea of the ecstatic character of spiritual presence gets an application far beyond the specific spirituality of the Christian faith, love, and hope which it was designed for. Instead of pointing to a peculiarity of Christian experience, it turns out representing a basic element of reality and particularly of organic life.

Revising Teilhard

The proposed revision of Teilhard's conception of evolution meets a number of the most serious arguments against his thought. Especially it permits the abandonment of the idea of a teleological guidance of the evolutionary process and the giving of much more importance to the element of chance or contingency in shaping that process. But is it really justifiable to use the term "spirit" in order to designate the energy working in the evolutionary process? Has such a description any theological significance? Is there any substantial continuity with the way in which the Christian tradition referred to the spirit of God as the creative origin of all life?

I shall discuss this question by asking first for the conditions for an adequate translation of the biblical idea of a creative spirit as origin of all life into the context of modern thought. Such an explanation will provide certain criteria, and these criteria can be applied afterward to Teilhard's ideas and to the model that emerged from our discussion of them.

Every attempt for a translation of ideas has first to consider the gulf that should be bridged. Most of the differences between the biblical and the modern understanding of life can be derived from the fact that the biblical idea of life works with the assumption of an origin of life that transcends the living being, as it was empirically evident to the ancient world in the phenomenon of breath, while the modern biological science conceives of life as function of the living cell that reproduces itself. At a first glance, this comparison gives the impression of a strict opposition between the modern immanentistic view of life and the explanation of life by a transcendent principle as it was offered by the Old Testament. Compared with this basic opposition, the identification of that transcendent principle as spirit appears to be of secondary importance. A closer look, however, reveals that there is more than that apparent opposition. On the one hand, the biblical perspective is quite open for the idea of independent existence which constitutes the very essence of the concept of a living being: it has life in itself. On the other hand, modern biology does not exclude everything that transcends the living cell from the analysis of life. Although life is taken as the activity of the living cell or of a higher organism, that activity itself is conditioned. It is conditioned particularly by the requirement of an appropriate environment. When kept in isolation, no organism is fit for life. In this sense, every organism depends on specific conditions for its life, and these conditions do not remain extrinsic to its own reality but contribute to the character of its life: an organism lives "in" its environment. It not only needs and actively occupies a territory but it turns it into a means for its self-realization, it nourishes itself on its environment. In this sense, every organism lives beyond itself. Again it becomes evident that life is essentially ecstatic: it takes place in the environment of the organism much more than in itself.

But is there any relation of this ecological self-transcendence of life to the biblical idea of a spiritual origin of life? I think there is. In order to recognize this correspondence we must first focus what has been said about the phenomenal character of spirit and keep in suspense for the time being the divine nature of the spirit. Then it becomes evident that breath belongs to the most important environmental conditions of life. Only if there is fresh air can the organic processes go on. Hence breath can be taken as an appropriate illustration of the dependence of the organism on its environment. To be sure, breath can no longer be regarded as the proper cause of life. At this point, every modern account of life has to confess its difference from the primitive explanation of life that was equaled also in the biblical writings. There is, however, an element of truth in that primitive explanation, and the first clue to it is to be found in the dependence of the organism on its environment.

It would be hardly defensible of course to maintain that an organism is created by its environment, although an appropriate environment is a necessary condition for its existence. But there is still another aspect of its living beyond itself: by turning its environment into the place and means of its life, the organism relates itself at the same time to its own future and, more precisely, to a future of its own transformation. This is true of every act of self-creation and nourishing and developing itself, by regenerating and reproducing its life. By its drives an animal is related to, although not necessarily aware of, its individual future and to the future of its species. This also belongs to the ecstatic character of the self-transcendence of life, and this is what Teilhard de Chardin called radial energy. It comes to most emphatic expression in the increasing complexity and final convergence of the evolutionary process of life, but it is present even in the life of the individual and specifically in the temporal aspect of the individual's self-transcendence. Now, if it was correct to revise Teilhard's account of radial energy in terms of a field of energy that shapes a process of evolution, then it makes sense also to maintain that this field of energy manifests itself in the self-transcendence of the living being, and thereby it even creates the lives of the individuals. Hence, the element of truth in the old image of breath as being the creative origin of life is not exhausted by the dependence of the organism on its environment, but contains a deeper mystery closely connected with the ecological self-transcendence of life: the temporal self-transcendence of every living being is a specific phenomenon of organic life that separates it from inorganic structures.

At this point, a number of questions arise that would deserve further investigation. In the first place, there is a question concerning the relation between ecology and genetics. The argument for the self-transcendence of life has been developed largely on the basis of ecological evidence. Does it also apply to genetics? If this were not so, the assumption of a field of energy effective in the self-transcendence of life would lose much of its persuasion. A second question concerns the character of that field itself: Is it legitimate to use the concept of a field when the impact of the future on the present is at stake, as it is the case with Teilhard's point Omega and with his assertion of a creative influence of Omega on the entire evolutionary process? Applied in such a way, the concept of a field replaces the age-old teleological language. Does it really fit that purpose? In any case, the temporal structure of field theories needs to be further investigated, especially in the light of the problems of the quantum theory that no longer abstracts from the question of time as other field theories do. This also involves the element of contingency in the effectiveness of such a field. Finally, granted the possibility of speaking about the creative effectiveness of Teilhard's point Omega in terms of a field of energy, its relevance for the phenomenon of spirit is still to be explained.

The Self-Transcendence of Life

The discussion of Tillich's and Teilhard's views on spirit and life resulted in the proposal of using the self-transcendence of life as a clue to the phenomenon of the spirit and as a basis for a redefinition of spiritual reality. This proposal owes part of its inspiration to Tillich's idea of the ecstatic character of "spiritual presence," but it does not follow his separation of that ecstatic experience from the process of life that is ultimately nourished on self-transcendence. Tillich accepted a separation of his idea of spiritual presence from the continuously self-transcending process of life, because he conceived of self-transcendence only in terms of an activity of the organism. But after the discussion of Teilhard's ideas of spirit and energy and particularly after having replaced Teilhard's "radial energy" by the assumption of a field of energy effective in the evolutionary process, we can conceive of self-transcendence in a more complex way: self-transcendence is to be regarded at the same time as an activity of the organism and as an effect of a power that continuously raises the organism beyond its limitations and thereby grants it its life. The functions of the self-creation and self-integration of life depend on the ongoing process of its self-transcendence. If the self-transcendent tendency of life could be exhaustively explained in terms of an autonomous activity of the organism, there would be no room left for the assumption of a spiritual reality involved in his life.

The term "spirit" in its broad application to the total sphere of life refers to the fact that the self-transcending activity of organic life is to be explained within a broader context as it is provided by the process of evolution toward a definitive self-assertion of life, but also by its abundant production of fragmentary symbols of the power and beauty of life, the results of its self-creative and self-integrative activity that anticipates the final goal of the evolutionary process.

The redefinition of the concept of spirit on the basis of the self-transcending tendency in all organic life unties the association of spirit with mind. Spirit is not identical with mind, nor is it manifested primarily through mind. Rather, the reflective nature of the human mind represents a particular form and degree of participation in the spiritual power, and that is closely connected with the particular mode of human self-transcendence.

We of the human race do not only live beyond ourselves in our environment and on its supplies. We do not in fact only change the environment by claiming it as our own. But we are able deliberately to change our world in order to change the conditions for our own existence. That presupposes first that we are able to consider the realities of our world on their own terms, not only in relation to our drives. We can be "with" the things different from ourselves in a way no other animal can. The second presupposition of the deliberate transformation of the world by human activity is that we are able to project a future in distinction from our present. That makes us master of the present. Both these aspects imply that we humans can take a stand beyond ourselves and look at ourselves from a distance. In other words, we have the capacity for reflection. The continuously reflective consciousness of the human being emphatically illustrates our particular mode of being beyond ourselves. And precisely in being beyond ourselves we are ourselves, not only as individuals but as humanity. In taking a stand beyond itself, the human mind is no longer itself the unity of experience, but is looking for something beyond itself that gives unity to experiences. We apprehend the particular only within a wider horizon of meaning which is anticipated as some sort of unity. This underlies all processes of abstract thinking. But the unity beyond the individual is also concrete in form of a community of individuals. Hence in the reflective consciousness of humanity the importance of social life for the individual develops to a new level: the social community in its difference from individual existence becomes constitutive for the individual's experience of the unity and identity of one's existence. In this particular way the human is a social being, not simply as a member of the flock, but by recognizing the community as manifesting a unity of human nature superior to one's individuality. Since, however, the society is composed of individuals, the final basis of its unity is to be asked for beyond the concrete institutions of social life: as social being, the human being is at the same time the religious being.

It is obvious that the particular mode of human self-transcendence characterizes all the specifically spiritual activities and achievements of the human race. It comes to expression in the human ability for conceiving abstract ideas as well as in trust, love, and hope. It is basic for the quest of the individual for personal identity as well as for one's social life and its institutions, and last but not least for one's creation of a world of meaning by developing language and by creating a world of culture. In all this, we are at the same time creative and receptive of the spiritual reality that raises us beyond ourselves. The most creative acts of our spiritual activity provide the most impressive evidence for this assertion: the creative design of an artist, the sudden discovery of a truth, the experience of being liberated for a moment of significant existence, the power of a moral commitment—all this comes to us by a sort of inspiration. All these experiences testify to a power that raises our hearts, the power of the spirit. When we are most creative, we most self-consciously participate in the spiritual power beyond ourself. But its presence does not only characterize the exceptional moments of elevation but it also permeates the general structure of human behavior in its openness beyond itself. The exceptional experiences of spiritual freedom and creativity illuminate the general condition of human existence.

Yet, human life is not yet fully united to the spirit. There are the hours when we live in low spirits or even let ourselves be taken in by a bad spirit. There are the occasions when we sadly realize the absence of true unity and meaning from our lives. There are the conflicts, repression, and violence among individuals and in the relations between the individual and the individual's social world. There is failure and guilt, disability, disease, and death. There are flashes of meaning, but only in a fragmentary way, and the wholeness of life remains an open question at the moment of death. There is, indeed, ample space for the ambiguities of human life, the dialectic that Paul Tillich so eloquently described. In the face of all this, the presence of loving concern, of mutual trust, of meaning and hope is almost a supernatural event, especially if it constitutes a continuous identity and integrity of our lives in spite of all its precariousness. In this way the Christian proclamation, with its assurance of a new life that will be no more subject to death, communicates a new and undisturbed confidence, a new and continuous spiritual presence. Its very heart lies in the confidence of being united to the future of God, a confidence that became incarnate in the existence of Christ and is effective in human history from that time on. The spirit, however, of this new spiritual presence that is a life in the community of faith, is no other spirit than the spirit that animates and quickens all life. Only because it is the same spirit that created all life by inspiring its abundant self-transcendence, it provides no escapist opiate, but the power of sustaining to and finally overcoming the absurdities and adversities of the present world.

6
Spirit and Energy

*The Phenomenology
of Teilhard de Chardin*

In his celebrated preface to *The Phenomenon of Man*, Pierre Teilhard de Chardin has given the most pregnant and distinctive description of his method. He wishes to limit himself to the "phenomenon" of human being. With this limitation to the phenomenon he separates himself from metaphysical analyses that probe behind the phenomenon, and therefore he can designate his work as natural science. To be sure, Teilhard is absolutely clear about the fact that he actually goes beyond the limits of the normal procedures of natural science. His goal appears to be physics in the Greek sense, which views humanity and nature together, over against the causal-analytic procedures of natural science. He calls this physics ultra-physics or hyper-physics.[1] But he seeks this physics on the same level on which empirical research is located as "the broadening and deepening of physics upon the same level of 'phenomenon.' "[2] The tendency toward such broadening comes to expression in the demand to comprehend not only part of a phenomenon but the phenomenon as a whole.[3]

The Inner "Within" of a Thing

In Teilhard's phenomenology the supposition of a "Within of the thing" is a particularly instructive example for the relationship of subject and object, humanity and nature. This is not a matter of an arbitrary example but the decisive weak point in his understanding of evolution, a point that must be clarified. Teilhard arrives at his thesis through the application of the principle "to discover behind the exception the universal truth."[4] The exception in this case is the fact of consciousness, which, according to our observation, appears clearly only among human beings amidst the entire expanse of nature. In order to comprehend the principle—namely, to comprehend each exception as "the emerging of a quality that has existed everywhere in an incomprehensible state"—causes Teilhard in addition to use the self-experience of humanity as the key to the understanding of nature and to ascribe to all phenomena a hidden "Within" by analogy to the human consciousness.

Teilhard therewith goes beyond the boundary of natural scientific thought, since the general supposition at which he arrives is no longer empirically determinable but can be judged only by its ability to give a unified picture of phenomena. From a strictly scientific standpoint Teilhard's method must in fact appear as a massive extrapolation in which the subjection of consciousness to the presence of the central nervous system is disregarded in favor of a more general relationship between gradations of consciousness and gradations of complexity of organization.[5] Yet the relevance of the thesis of Teilhard as the broadening of the natural scientific way of thinking in a strict sense for a natural philosophy is not shaken by the criticism of empirical natural science. The limitation of our form of consciousness to functions of the brain need not exclude the thesis that something analogous to our consciousness, though not exactly like it, is supposed also to exist there where as yet no central nervous system is present. Such suppositions have obtruded themselves again and again where one can neither be content with the Cartesian dualism of *res extensa* and *res cogitans* nor explain consciousness as mere epiphenomenon of an entirely heterogeneous material occurrence. The supposition that human consciousness as an element of the specifically human form of life represents a modification of a more universal characteristic of all natural phenomena in general, which appears as a condition of the continuity of the unity of nature which is also inclusive of humanity, even when this assumption of an empirical judgment is avoided or when such a one in any case at first cannot be made.

Teilhard does not stand alone with this idea but is ranked in a long philosophical tradition with other panpsychists. The modern form of this line of thinking is linked above all with Leibniz's monadology in which all monads were conceived as something analogous to the mind. Leibniz wanted to reserve the designation "mind" for the essence given in perception[6] and the form of experience of the lower monads as perception, though distinguished from the human consciousness designated as apperception.[7] More recently panpsychism has appeared in the various forms of process philosophy in which one must also rank Teilhard. In Henri Bergson, to whom Teilhard remains so frequently linked in spite of the contrast of his "creative union" with the progressively driven *élan vital* of "creative evolution," panpsychism is limited, to be sure, to the realm of the living in contrast to inanimate matter.[8] So Teilhard's thought at this point stands closer to the philosophy of Alfred North Whitehead. Though Whitehead has not explicitly spoken also of a "Within" of phenomena, his thought remains still pertinent to such an idea when he translates subjectivity in the process of human experience to all natural events. Whitehead conceives consciousness as characteristic of each elementary event, of every actual occasion.[9] This becomes especially clear when he says that in each event of self-constitution we find, in addition to the physical pole of its experience, also a mental pole and a subjective aim.[10] He can therefore already recognize a principle of reason in all natural occurrences.[11] Be that as it may, we ought not to overlook the fact that Whitehead attributed mind in the true sense only to human beings and the higher animals;[12] and he held consciousness to be a later, derived product of a complex process of integration.[13] The difference between Teilhard and Whitehead is primarily a terminological one, conditioned by a more narrow idea of consciousness.

Spiritual Energy

With the supposition of a "Within of the thing," which is analogous to the human consciousness, respectively, to the human mind,[14] Teilhard stands therefore in a broad tradition of natural philosophy that goes back ultimately to Plato's idea of a world soul. The relationship of this idea to the concept of energy as Teilhard conceives it is less general. He proceeds from the idea of a spiritual energy in Bergson's sense—which he presupposes as familiar—and inquires into its relation to the concept of energy in physics. His own hypothesis follows from the supposition that really every kind of energy is psychic in nature, but that this basic energy appears in two ways in phenomena—namely, on the one hand, in the relationship of bodies of a similar order with one another (tangential energy) and, on the other hand, in the transcendence of the self toward increasing complexity and centration (radial energy).[15]

The fundamental concept of the essential psychic nature of all energy is thus expressed in the distinction between tangential energy and radial energy. From the supposition that energy belongs together with the "Within of the thing," the distinction of two kinds of energy, which indeed finds no support in natural scientific language, becomes understandable. One needs only to add that each "Within" expresses itself in the external structures of phenomena. It manifests itself, according to Teilhard, in the interrelationships between bodies. In particular, concerning energy, it is a matter of the "power of union" (*pouvoir de liaison*), which "concentrates and unites the particles with one another."[16] This "solidarity" of the corporeal elements is comprehensible in their interrelations and therefore in the manifested form of their movement. This is the energy of the physicist, for whom, as Teilhard says, at least until today, there is "only a 'Without' of the thing."[17] If, however, energy as regards its nature is psychic, then it cannot be exhausted in this aspect in which it becomes externally comprehensible. Therefore psychic energy[18] in the strict sense is distinguished from every outwardly constituted tangential energy that Teilhard finds on the road of evolution toward ever-increasing complexity and he designates psychic energy as radial energy.

The peculiarity of this method becomes completely clear, then, when one makes clear which aspect of the concept of energy in Teilhard's description remains overlooked. It is a matter in particular of the field nature of energy. Classical mechanics has to do with bodies, with respect to their position in space and time as well as with the forces operating between bodies. Classical physics attempted to reduce the multiplicity of forces and to relate the concept of force generally to the qualities of bodies, in particular to their mass.[19] This attempt had been undertaken for one last time still by Albert Einstein. However, instead of breaking up Newtonian space into qualities and relations of bodies, relativity theory has actually made space itself as a field into a physical object, so that it is now suggested that matter be conceived as a quality of space.[20] Thus, the final turn was made from a bodily oriented concept of energy to one of an independently standing energy now thought of as a field over against bodies.[21]

The radicality of this shift of the concept of energy from one of a property of bodies to the idea of the field applied to bodies by which the singular materialization is finally to be understood as the body itself is not itself operable in Teilhard's concept of energy. To be sure, Teilhard by all means recognized in energy the essential "fundamental principle" of physics, and even the basis of the physical concept of energy in the interrelations between bodies is discernible when he specifies the "reality of collective relations" as the physical place of energy—or its "tangential" form of manifestation.[22] However, it is not by chance that the field concept plays no part for Teilhard.[23] While he connects energy with the "Within of the thing," the idea of the body remains the data point for his conception of energy.[24] To be sure, the body is only the exterior side of that to which in its inner essence corresponds to energy. However, energy as the Within represents itself here only by this exterior and therefore as something inherent to the body itself. Yet the energy that is able itself to go beyond the individual and the species is described in this point of view as belonging to this phenomenon and going out from it, instead of standing independently over against it as a self-transcending power and effect. This problem of "radial energy" constitutes the hard kernel of finalism in Teilhard's concept of orthogenesis. The idea of a "systematically planned complexification," of a "determined orientation of life" by "a favored axis of evolution," lies already in the concept of radial energy insofar as it tends toward increasing complexity.

The category of orthogenesis has been impugned because it allegedly implies a teleological consequence in the sense of a final indication of the development out of which the substance of life develops itself.[25] But when Teilhard advocates the concept of orthogenesis he does not decide for "an out of date vitalistic or finalistic conception" that misinterprets orthogenesis as "so to speak, a magic linearity of phyla."[26] That is not to say that he in general rejects every final sense of orthogenesis; rather, he expressly designates his conception as finalistic.[27] Teilhard defends himself only against a finalism that would give no place to the role of chance. Therefore he offers a statistical interpretation of the concept. First of all, he indicates the appearance of a statistical center within the chance distribution of morphological variations. In looking back, the statistical distribution appears to him then, however, as a self-grouping of species; "rather, under the effect of a large number they tend on their part to group themselves within a known conical structure."[28] The statistical phenomenon is tied to the subject of an inner aspiration—an aspiration that is extrapolated to apply to evolution in its entirety, as the tendency to go beyond human evolution to Omega.[29] The element of finalism enters into consideration by interpreting the statistical as an expression of the organism or species. Thereby the relationship of energy to the moving parts of bodies clearly returns. If radial energy is considered as the Within of phenomena, as the character of energy itself through which it transcends itself and tends toward increasing complexity, then, one may add that even the statistical discovery of the disproportionate distribution of morphological variations can be conceived as the expression of a tendency and self-grouping of species.

Teilhard's Contradiction

By way of this finalistic notion that is found in his concept of energy, Teilhard falls into contradiction with the central intention of his conception of God. From many of his lines of argumentation, it appears as if point Omega is introduced and postulated as a final extrapolation and completion of the evolutionary process;[30] however, Teilhard's ultimate intention moves toward thinking of Omega (or in any case the transcendental side of Omega[31]) as the Prime Mover, as an auto-center and a creative cause of evolution in its independence over against the process of evolution.[32]

This intuition that the end is the true beginning is found in Teilhard's earlier discussion of Bergson when he contrasts the *vis a tergo* of the *élan vital*, "a thrust of life without finality," to the idea of a *vis ab ante*, a power of the future; "the power that creates the world can only be a *vis ab ante*, a uniting power."[33] The concept of a uniting power allows the recognition that Teilhard still thinks of the power of the future in the sense of the Aristotelian Prime Mover.[34] Beyond that, however, and thereby the creative work of God comes in view to him, Teilhard thinks of the power of God as a power creating unit. Thus, already included in every early outline, and after 1948 in "*Comment je vois*," the same thought returns again deeper: "To create is to unite."

How can this energy, however, be related to the energy that is concerned with the Within of material phenomena? Is it finally identical with it? How can it, however, then be ascribed to the phenomena themselves as their Within and as going out from them? Does Teilhard perhaps remain more committed to the *vis a tergo* (that was certainly not only Bergson's concept of energy but also that of classical mechanics) than accords with his vision of "creative union"?

If evolution is thought of as an expression of energies that are inherent to bodies and that incite its striving "to go" beyond itself, then Omega is at most conceivable as the extrapolated perfection of their efficacy but not as the creative origin of evolution. Vice versa, if Omega as the power of the future shapes the creative origin of evolution, then the energy that moves this process is not to be understood already by itself as the energy dwelling in the phenomena. Rather, Omega is that which transcends itself so that the independent standing of energy as a field over against its connection to bodies is made possible. What Teilhard says in *"Comment je vois"* about consciousness as a consequence of the supposition of Omega was to apply in the same sense to all phases and aspects of cosmic evolution:

> that the tide of consciousness of which we form a part is not produced simply by some impulse that originates in ourselves. It feels the pull of a star, upon which, individually and as one whole, we are completing in union our process of self-interiorization. (Paragraph 24)

Teilhard has described the creative, unifying effect of Omega through the concept of spirit, although (to my knowledge) he nowhere concerns himself about the relation of the presence of spirit to the futurity of Omega.[35] Insofar as it is a matter, the power of concentration[36] and convergence[37] in regard to spirit takes place in the process of spiritualization in no other way than by the creative presence of Omega in the process of evolution. Already the "Creative Union" of 1917 includes in the process of "spiritualization" through becoming one, "the spiritual substance," that is, "the unified center itself."[38] Here spirit is not understood on the basis of consciousness, but, vice versa, consciousness is understood on the basis of the unifying power of spirit. *The Divine Milieu* (1927) describes in peculiarly religious language the same facts. It was formulated most significantly in the German translation of "The Phenomenon of Spirituality" (1937), namely, "the conscious beings, whose spirits are described here as the various pointed manifestations of a Greater that encompasses all," namely, as manifestations of the characteristic *one* spirit whose unity is to be grasped as a sphere, as Noosphere.[39] Obviously, this sphere is related to the individual centers of consciousness as the field is related to the singular bodies in which it manifests itself. This comparison is all the more obvious when Teilhard turns expressly to begin his essay against the separation of spirit and earthly energy with the remark that the spirit

> quite simply represents the higher state assumed in and around us by the primal and indefinable thing that we call, for want of a better name, the "stuff of the universe." . . . Spirit is neither a meta- nor an epi-phenomenon; it is *the* phenomenon.[40]

Notes

1. Pierre Teilhard de Chardin, *The Phenomenon of Man* (New York: Harper & Brothers, 1959). Cf. Karl Schmitz-Moorman, *Das Weltbild Teilhard de Chardins*, vol. 1: *Physik—Ultraphysik—Metaphysik: Untersuchungen zur Terminologie Teilhard de Chardins* (Köln/Opladen, 1966).
2. Sigurd M. Daecke, *Teilhard de Chardin und die evangelische Theologie* (1967), 263.
3. Therewith, Teilhard turns against the phenomenology of both Husserl and Merleau-Ponty (cf. A. Gosztonyi, *Der Mensch und die Evolution* [1968], 21ff.) and also against the methodological restrictions of the exact natural sciences.
4. Pierre Teilhard de Chardin, *Der Mensch im Kosmos*, 2d ed. (Munich, 1959), 31.
5. Thus, N. A. Luyten, *Teilhard de Chardin: Eine neue Wissenschaft?* (Freiburg/Munich, 1966), 30ff.
6. G. W. Leibniz, *Monadologie*, par. 19. Cf. also the letter to Bierling of December 8, 1711 (Gerhardt, 7:502 zit. nach PhB 253, 70).
7. Ibid., par. 14.
8. Henri Bergson, *L'évolution créatrice* (Paris: Presses Universitaire de France, 1948), 187. See also Bergson, *L'énergie spirituelle* (Paris, 1967), 8 as well as pp. 199ff. in *L'évolution créatrice*, where Bergson also speaks (p. 200), however, of inner and living unity of everything in nature. M. Barthélemy-Madaule, *Bergson und Teilhard de Chardin* (Olten, 1970), sees in Bergson's restriction of panpsychism to the dualism of life and matter a point of difference with regard to Teilhard (pp. 334ff., also pp. 307ff.). The point of difference is not great. A point of departure from the self-phenomenon of man, from consciousness, applies not only to Bergson but still yet to Teilhard, as his basis for the supposition of a "Within of the thing" in the human phenomenon shows, that generalizes the fact of human consciousness to a higher level (against Barthélemy-Madaule, 273ff.). On the other side, the relation of grades of consciousness to the level of complexity of organic structures and especially to their nervous systems is already found in Bergson (*L'évolution créatrice*, 252ff.).
9. Alfred North Whitehead, *Process and Reality* (New York: Harper & Brothers, Harper Torchbooks, 1957), 28ff. and 252ff. There Whitehead conceives the idea of experience in a broader sense than that of consciousness: "Consciousness presupposes experience, and not experience consciousness" (p. 83). The primitive form of experience is prehension or feeling (on feeling, cf. p. 35). The broadening of the idea of experience by Whitehead is similar to Teilhard's result of generalization, a method that Whitehead perceived as constitutive for philosophical method (pp. 7f.)
10. On subjective aim, see Whitehead, *Process and Reality*, 29, 130ff., and 343. On mental pole, see ibid., 165, 366f., 379ff.
11. Alfred North Whitehead, *The Function of Reason* (1929; Boston: Beacon Press, 1958), 26ff., 32f.
12. Alfred North Whitehead, *Modes of Thought* (New York: G. P. Putnam's Sons, Capricorn Books, 1958), 231. Here as well as in *Process and Reality*, 163ff., Whitehead speaks of mentality.

13. Whitehead, *Process and Reality*, 245. Cf. R. H. Overman, *Evolution and the Christian Doctrine of Creation* (Philadelphia: Westminster Press, 1967), 220f.

14. See in addition the conception of consciousness and matter as "various aspects of the same reality" which is presented by C. F. von Weizsäcker, *Die Einheit der Natur* (Munich: Carl Hanser Verlag, 1971), 315ff., where mind is presented as the nonobjective background of embodied phenomena.

15. Teilhard de Chardin, *Der Mensch im Kosmos*, 40, 128. On the concept of energy, also see the description of Barthélemy-Madaule, *Bergson und Teilhard de Chardin*, 119ff., esp. 121ff., with the statement of the book concerning particularity of the human species of 1954 which in the present context, however, can remain outside our consideration.

16. Ibid., 16. In this emphasis of the unifying function over against the complementary function of expansion, the perspective of "creative union" could be expressed that perceives the theme of cosmic processes in the control of multiplicity.

17. Ibid., 30.

18. Ibid., 28.

19. Cf. C. F. von Weizsäcker, *Die Einheit der Physik* (1971), 136ff., 147f., 186ff.

20. See also Max Jammer, *Das Problem des Raumes: Die Entwicklung der Raumtheorien* (Darmstadt: Wissenschaftliche Buchgesellschaft, 1960), esp. 192ff., 212ff.

21. Einstein's attempt "to also understand bodies as singularities of fields of force" remains, however, chiefly a torso as von Weizsäcker (*Die Einheit der Physik*, 187) confirms, in which he did not include the quantum phenomena which in the meantime has been discovered. But, he goes on, "Today quantum theory is nearing the point at which it can take up again the conversation about Einstein's program," namely, upon the level of quantum field theory.

22. Teilhard de Chardin, *Der Mensch im Kosmos*, 16.

23. See the reserved opinion of Teilhard toward Einstein in his letter of October 7, 1930 (cited in Barthélemy-Madaule, *Bergson und Teilhard*, 750 n. 14). Obviously, Teilhard, the student of Bergson, is suspicious of the concept of field as a purely geometric construction which disregards the problem of time.

24. This is in Whitehead not the case, however, since he takes as the cause of his demand for a nonmaterialistic philosophy of natural science the inversion of the relationship of mass and energy, the retreat of the concept of matter behind that of the field of electrodynamics. See Alfred North Whitehead, *Science and the Modern World* (1925; New York: New American Library, 1960), 96ff. His answer was "We must start with the event as the ultimate unit of natural occurrence" (p. 97). Since Whitehead chose as the basis of his conception—not without parallel to the quantum theory which at that time was arising—the atomism of events and not the unity of energy or of fields, which surely manifests itself in events in a singular way, he has himself thereby established that "energy is merely the name for the quantitative aspect of a structure of happenings" (p. 96). Thus, however, no account is taken of the unity of energy in its opposing alleged reality, since it cannot be turned

back from the multiplicity of events in which it comes to appearance in phenomenon. Through the isolated emphasis on the quantification of energy, it is dissolved in Whitehead into the multiplicity of elementary events. See, however, on the contrary, the description of E. Schrödinger in his essay "Was ist ein Elementarteilchen?" (1962) toward a natural scientific view of life (pp. 121ff.).

25. So Barthélemy-Madaule, *Bergson und Teilhard*, 197ff., 183ff.

26. Toward the defense of orthogenesis in connection with the *Speziationsfiguren* (1955), *Werke*, 4:389ff., esp. 392ff.

27. Teilhard de Chardin, *Der Mensch im Kosmos*, 214.

28. Note concerning the actual reality and evolutive significance of human orthogenesis (1951), *Werke*, 4:361ff., esp. 363.

29. Ibid., 365f.; similarly, Teilhard de Chardin, *Der Mensch im Kosmos*, 146.

30. The concept of the supposition is expressly brought into relation with Omega in "*Comment je vois*" (1948), but the argument made there is found in many other texts; in particular, the argument for the irreversibility of evolution.

31. Pierre Teilhard de Chardin, "Entwurf einer Dialektik des Geistes" (1946), *Werke*, 7:26–36, esp. 29ff.

32. Ibid., 31.

33. Pierre Teilhard de Chardin, "Die schöpferische Einigung" (1917), in *Frühe Schriften* (Freiburg/Munich, 1968), 181ff., quoted on p. 192.

34. Teilhard de Chardin, "Entwurf einer Dialektik des Geistes" (1946), *Werke*, 7:30. One observes also the difficulty that Teilhard (p. 36) perceives with regard to the problem of thinking of God as efficient cause and not only as final cause—a problem with which already the Christian theology of the Middle Ages confronted with Aristotelianism when it wanted to think of God as creator of the world.

35. It appears that since the identity of Omega as the Ultimum of evolution with the Maximum of complexity and centration and, therefore, with the highest consciousness—"as a prime essence of absolute consciousness" (*Werke*, 6:147), Teilhard's thought all too quickly allows itself to enter into the course of a mediated apprehension of a divine consciousness which is not temporal and therefore does not concern the absolute future of God.

36. Teilhard de Chardin, "Das geistige Phänomen" (1937), *Werke*, 6:134.

37. Ibid., 136.

38. Teilhard de Chardin, *Frühe Schriften*, 188f.

39. *Werke*, 6:128.

40. Ibid., 126.

7

Spirit and Mind

The notion of spirit and reflections on the spiritual nature of the mind do not enjoy a place of particular prominence in the modern philosophical discussion of the concept of mind. This may be due to a deliberate avoidance of unwanted connotations reminding us of certain traditional beliefs in spiritual substances beside and behind the material world. It is the conjecture of this chapter, however, that a discussion of the difference and connections between mind and spirit may be helpful in exploring and clarifying the relationship between mind and body, which in recent years has become more of an open question again than many would have assumed some decades ago. Besides, a discussion of the difference and connection between mind and spirit enables theology to enter into the picture and dispute over mind and body and to contribute to the question concerning the place of mind in nature.

The obvious context of the mind-body problem in the history of modern thought is, of course, the Cartesian doctrine of two substances, *res cogitans* and *res extensa*. Karl Popper has shown that, on the basis of Descartes's theory of matter and of the mechanical movements of bodies, it became inexplicable how the immaterial soul could conceivably move the body.[1] He pointed out further how this difficulty gave rise to the various theories of a parallelism of mind and body, from the Occasionalists through Spinoza to Leibniz. The Cartesian dualism also became the occasion of the attempts of physicalism in proving the assumption of a second substance, mind, to be superfluous. In philosophy, this tendency was greatly promoted by David Hume's criticism of the conception of mind as a substance. While in the early days of British empiricism John Locke believed that the notion of mind as a special, spiritual substance arose from the operations we experience in ourselves, just as evidently as the notion of body arises from "those simple ideas we have from without,"[2] Hume considered the notion of mind as a particular substance to be "absolutely unintelligible," since he assured us that we have no impression of a mind comparable to the sense impressions that lead to perceptions of external objects.[3] Under the impact of physicalism and behaviorism the pressures toward a reduction of the notion of mind to functions and epiphenomena of bodily processes increased, and in recent decades philosophical language analysis contributed a further argument to the same result by reducing the self to a mode of speech, the "index word" I. Thus Gilbert Ryle, in his famous book on the concept of mind, could scoff at "the myth of the ghost in the machine." Hence, there was a great deal of surprise when Popper confessed to his belief in the ghost in the machine and, together with John Eccles, reformulated a dualist and interactionalist model of the relation between mind and body, especially between mind and brain on the basis of Eccles's neurological description of the human brain. The book they published together, *The Self and Its Brain*, reopened the discussion of the issue.[4]

Popper's main argument against physicalism or materialism is that, at least in the more radical forms of that interpretation of nature, not only the reality of consciousness is denied but especially the existence of technological artifacts and other objects of human culture cannot be accounted for in such a way as to do justice to their specifically logical structure and form of construction. Nor is physicalistic behaviorism able to account for the higher functions of language, that is, for its descriptive and argumentative functions.[5]

The positive complement of this critique of physicalism is the interpretation of the evolution of life and even of cosmic evolution in terms of a process of *emergence*,[6] where random events sometimes bring about a new epoch under the selective pressures of the environment. Emergent qualities, therefore, are something new and unpredictable. Following Alister Hardy's organic theory of evolution, Popper believes that in this way changes in behavior can also become selective factors in the evolutionary process.[7] This provides the general basis for his more specific thesis that linguistic behavior became a selective factor in the evolution of the human race: "The evolution of language can be explained, it seems, only if we assume that even a primitive language can be helpful in the struggle for life," and "Language, once created, exerted the selection pressure under which emerged the human brain and the consciousness of self."[8]

The emergence of self-consciousness, then, and of the self-conscious mind, is based on language rather than the other way round. This also applied to the development of the individual person: "We are not born as selves; but . . . we have to learn to be selves."[9] That is not only a matter of language. The acquisition of language presupposes the discovery of the world through perception and especially the development of a sense for the constancy of objects, of spatial relations, and for identity in time. But the culmination of all this is the learning of a language. Thus: "Temporally, the body is there before the mind. The mind is a later achievement."[10]

This view of the emergence of the self-conscious mind from language, and therefore from a sociocultural environment, calls to mind the thought of G. H. Mead, who also considered the self as arising from social interaction and especially from language. But Popper is more radical than Mead was. According to Popper's argument, it is not only some conception of ourselves but the human mind as such that arises from the social world and especially through the acquisition of language, although of course there are hereditary predispositions for such a process.

To me, this conjectural account for the emergence of self-consciousness seems highly suggestive. There are, of course, problems. One of these problems is that it becomes necessary to distinguish strictly between consciousness and self-consciousness, since language certainly presupposes sense perception. Indeed, in his dialogues with John Eccles, Popper repeatedly stressed that distinction between consciousness and self-consciousness, and he indicated at the same time that it is only self-consciousness that is to be considered a human privilege, while momentary consciousness in connection with perceptional activity should be attributed also to the higher animals.[11] The notion of mind, then, as emerging first from language, is to be strictly and intimately related to self-consciousness in distinction from consciousness in general.

Another problem appears in some places where Popper characterizes the world of culture and language—World 3, as he calls it— in terms of the world of the contents of thought and of "the products of the human mind."[12] What is the status of language in this context? If the human mind arises first through language, then it is certainly conceivable that some feedback of the human mind on the development and use of language may occur, but language as such cannot simply be described any longer as a product of the mind. Otherwise, the emergence of mind would be explained by a factor that itself takes its origin from mind. If the human mind first emerges through language, then in the origin of language there must be something prior to mind, but nevertheless also different from physical reality, since the distinction of the mind from physical reality is derived from it. The field, wherein the formation of language occurs, may be called a spiritual field. This does not seem inappropriate, because the terms "spiritual" and "spirit" should not be restricted to the religious life. There is a long-standing usage of the term "spirit" in relation to intellectual activities. But the religious dimension is also important. In the origins of human culture as well as in the development of the individual, the formulation of language seems closely related to the origins of religious awareness. If this is the field from where the mind emerges, it may be appropriately called a field of spiritual awareness.

The meaning of the word "spirit" has become vague and opaque in our secular culture. Its potential has to be recovered first, before it can be used. Therefore it is necessary to make explicit at least a few aspects of the spectrum of thought which is connected with the word "spirit" and may be present in its connotations.

In the history of Western philosophy, the notion of spirit has been often restricted more or less to the concept of mind. Thus, according to Locke, "The ideas we have belonging and peculiar to spirit, are thinking and will, or a power of putting body into motion by thought and, which is consequent to it, liberty." It is by "putting together the ideas of thinking and willing" that "we have the idea of an immaterial spirit,"[13] and therefore Locke attributed the "operations of the mind" to a "substance," which he called "spirit."[14] But as early as in Augustine, the term "spirit" was used as an equivalent to mind (*mens*),[15] and according to Thomas Aquinas, the human soul is called spiritual or spirit because of its intellectual potential.[16] However, Aquinas was still aware of a broader concept of spirit, which has an application even to material things and processes: it expresses the intuition of impulse and motion.[17] It was a late echo of this broader concept of spirit, when in the eighteenth and early nineteenth centuries, spirit was taken as the animating principle of life,[18] before in Hegel's thought the power of spirit was bound up with the dynamics of concept and idea and the post-Hegelians reduced it again to the individual mind.

The most important source of that broader concept of spirit was undoubtedly the Bible, where spirit—the spirit of God—is conceived in analogy to the dynamics of the wind (John 3:8; cf. Gen. 1:2; Ezek. 37:9f.) and is understood as the principle of life: According to Psalm 104, it is the spirit of God who renews the surface of the ground in springtime, and all creatures die, when God takes away the share of the spirit given to them (Ps. 104:29f.). In a similar way, according to the older story of the creation of man, God breathes the "breath of life" into his nostrils (Gen. 2:7). It is only this breath of life which makes the human body a "living being" or, more literally, a "living soul" (Gen. 2:7). Elsewhere, this breath of life is identified as the divine spirit (*ruach*), which is given by God and returned to him when the human person dies (Eccles. 12:7), just as the Gospel of Luke reports that Jesus died with the words of Ps. 31:5: "Father, into your hands I commend my spirit" (Luke 23:46). The conception of the divine spirit as origin of life comes to powerful expression in the prophet Ezekiel's vision of the resurrection of the dead, strongly reminiscent of the origin of human life according to the Genesis story: "The dry bones of the people of Israel come alive when the wind or spirit from God breathes into them" (Ezek. 37:5f. and 10, cf. v. 14).[19] It is in the line of these ideas that the famous words of the apostle Paul are to be understood that, while the first Adam was created a living being (according to Gen. 2:7), the last Adam became life-giving spirit: "Therefore the body of the risen Lord and of those who will be raised with him is a spiritual body" (1 Cor. 15:45). In the context of the Old Testament thought about spirit and life, the notion of a spiritual body can only mean that there will be a form of life that is no longer separate from the divine spirit, the origin of life, but remains in unity with that origin. Therefore Paul expects the new life of the resurrection to be immortal (1 Cor. 15:53ff.). In distinction from this hope for life in unity with God, the present life is not immortal, because it does not stay in unity with God, although it also owes its origin to God's life-giving spirit. This is Paul's idea of a "living being" in the present order of reality: it originates from the divine spirit, the giver of all life, but it is a separate reality departing from that origin and therefore mortal. It is within this framework that one has to interpret other distinctions of the apostle between the human and the divine, between human spirit or mind (*nous*) and the spirit of God (1 Cor. 2:11f.; cf. 1 Cor. 14:14f.).

The Pauline reinterpretation of the place of the divine spirit in biblical anthropology became an important subject in early patristic thought. The discussions of the Christian fathers took place in an intellectual climate, where the Stoic concept of a divine *pneuma*, pervading the cosmos and manifest in the logical nature of the human soul, came close to the biblical ideas of the life-giving spirit of God, and the later Platonic idea of the divine character of the *nous* or mind converged to a certain degree with the Genesis account of the creation of the human soul by the breath of God's spirit. The Gnostics combined the Genesis account and Platonism to the effect that they considered the human soul of the chosen ones as participating in the divine nature of the *pneuma* from the moment of creation. The church fathers, on the other hand, considered participation in the divine *pneuma* as a matter of salvation rather than of creation. The natural human person, even his or her mind, has no share in the divine spirit. Nevertheless, the fathers had to admit that the created mind is related to and its life is constituted by the creative presence of God's spirit. The human mind is in need of being illumined by the divine spirit, and its disposition for the spirit is fully actualized only through salvation, through the pouring out of God's spirit into the hearts of the faithful, whether in the act of baptism— as Clement of Alexandria thought—or in the process of sanctification which only starts with baptism, according to the teaching of Origen.[20] But even in those in whom the divine spirit takes permanent dwelling, the spirit does not become part of their nature but moves and activates them by his divine power.[21]

According to Christian patristics, then, there always remains a difference between the mind—which is sometimes called the human spirit—and the divine spirit. This is a somewhat restrictive interpretation of the biblical words that speak of a share of the human soul in the spirit of God. It is a limited share, of course, because human life, like all living creatures, is under the power of death. This limitation was emphasized by Paul in contrast to the life to come, which will be permanently united to the life-giving spirit. Patristic theology also was anxious to emphasize the limitations of the natural human being's natural share in the spirit, because the church fathers considered the endowment with the spirit's presence an achievement peculiar to salvation. But they admitted that a special kinship exists, indeed, between the human soul and God's spirit, and they went beyond the Pauline statements in attributing that kinship specifically to the mind. Thus, not only does the mind originate from God's spirit, as all living beings do, but it is also disposed to receive the illumination of the spirit in different stages up to the permanent indwelling of the spirit in the human soul.

All this, of course, is history. Does it have any significance for the interpretation of contemporary experience? Can the distinctive and dynamic interrelation of mind and spirit serve as a model, as a source of inspiration, when it comes to the contemporary problems of understanding the function of mind, its origin, and its relation to the human body and brain? In such a way the theologian should use biblical materials and conceptualities as well as the Christian teaching of the past. They should be treated not as dogmatic definitions but as a source of inspiration for an appropriate understanding of present experience. Certain models derived from this tradition may be refuted by present experience. Still, the theologian will continue to look to the Bible and to the teaching of the church in confidence that from the wealth of that tradition, further clues for more adequate solutions of the problems may be obtained.

One possible advantage of interpreting the dependence of mind on the cultural process in general and on language in particular in terms of a spiritual origin of mind was mentioned before we set out to recover from history the latent potential of the notion of spirit in relation to the human soul. Such an interpretation could help to avoid a vicious circle in explaining the origin of mind by reference to culture and language, while culture and language in their turn are commonly understood to be products of the mind. But now, after some clarifications of the concept of spirit have been obtained, it becomes doubtful whether its meaning really applies to the problem of mind and language, of mind and culture. First of all, the biblical notion of spirit is related to the understanding of life and to the question of its origin, not primarily to human culture. However, certain extraordinary cultural achievements, especially the work of the artist, are said to require an extraordinary endowment with the divine spirit (Ex. 28:3; 31:3; 35:31), just as the achievement of heroes and the responsibilities of social leaders, especially of the king. Further, in this category belongs the charisma of the prophet, of the poet, and of the wise elder. The vision of the prophet, as well as his words, comes from divine inspiration. But do these extraordinary phenomena admit the generalized assertion that all cultural phenomena and especially language in general indicate the presence and activity of the divine spirit in the human person? It seems that the statement in the older creation story about the endowment of Adam with the divine spirit does indeed present us with such a generalization. It is true, the story speaks of the breath of life. But on the other hand, it is the distinction of the human person from other creatures that is expressed that way. The creation story does not explicitly relate the divine endowment of Adam with the breath of life to the phenomenon of language, which is mentioned only later, when the story tells that God brought the animals he created to Adam in order "to see what he would call them; and whatever the man called every living creature, that was its name" (Gen. 2:19). Language is described here as a human invention, as Johann Gottfried von Herder insisted, rather than as a supernatural gift of God, but one must not forget that the constitution of the human soul by the divine breath of life stands at the beginning of this story. Human invention and divine inspiration are not mutually exclusive, but divine inspiration activates the spiritual power of the human mind.

In the contemporary discussion, the relation between language and religion is rarely given the attention the phenomenon deserves. The dialogues between John Eccles and Karl Popper on mind and its origin are no exception in this respect. They mention a few times the myth-making activity of the human mind alongside other cultural activities, but they do not assign a special function to it comparable, say, to Ernst Cassirer's theory of symbolic forms. Cassirer saw myth at the origins of language, although language as we know it is no longer a magical incantation of reality. That mystical origin of language seems to be of special importance for the descriptive function of human language, which Popper stresses as the distinctively human element in language. The naming of an object is originally an ecstatic event, because in its name the object itself is thought to be present.[22] This hypothesis of Cassirer's has been corroborated by certain findings of Jean Piaget in his research on the acquisition of language in the intellectual development of children. Piaget found that the early development of language is intimately related to play where the real object is represented symbolically by the toy, and he also found "mythical" and "animistic" elements in the intuitive thinking and talking of children until their seventh year.[23] Moreover, Piaget emphasizes the function of these phenomena in the acquisition of an awareness of an objective world, within which the child's own body and person take their place. All this is the more remarkable in view of the fact that Piaget does not only refer to Cassirer in this connection but has no intention of developing anything like a theory of a religious origin of language. He need not think of such an explanation, because he is accustomed to talking as if the child were a subject in its own right almost from the day of birth. This would presuppose that the human mind is already there from birth so that all experiences could be explained as actions of that subject. But if the human mind is no substance or primordial subject of our experiences, but emerges only in the course of our discovery of the world around us, especially of the social and cultural world, as Popper suggests, so that the mind is comparable to the phenomenon of a flame that nourishes itself from the combustible material within its reach, then the origin of the self-conscious mind itself has to be looked for in the early acquisition of that world, and then, as far as language is concerned, the mythical and religious spirituality in the process of acquiring language becomes important. Such a spirituality may have surrounded also the first origins of language in the history of the human race.[24] Certain peculiarities of language, especially in its descriptive function, are better explained in such a perspective than on the assumption that language was formed in the service of toolmaking or hunting.[25]

The biblical concept of the divine spirit as origin of mind seems particularly interesting in relation to another problem connected with the descriptive function of language: How does one explain the fact that human mind and language are fit to grasp the reality of things as they really are? The possibility of truth in human statements would cause no great problem, if the human mind were completely passive and receptive in its perceptions. But today we know that, on the contrary, the mind and the brain are active in every moment of experience, starting with sense perception. How is it possible that nevertheless the information we receive from the outside is not hopelessly distorted? On the basis of the biblical conception of spirit and mind, the answer could be that the same spirit that the human mind shares is also the origin of "life" in the beings outside ourselves, the creative origin of their particular "gestalt." Something like this may underlie the enigmatic remark in the creation story that "whatever the man called every living creature, that was its name" (Gen. 2:19). If we recall that to the archaic mind the name of a thing comprises its nature, this biblical phrase means nothing less than that the human person, on the basis of his or her participation in the divine spirit, is able to grasp the nature of things. Here it becomes important that the concept of spirit functions not only as origin of mind. Precisely because the spirit is the source of life at large, it can become the origin of mind, too, that grasps the reality of all "living beings."

The range of the mind's perceptive power extends beyond the living beings to everything real, although it may have a special affinity to the nature of organisms, since the human mind is itself a "living soul" (Gen. 2:7). The explanation of the intelligibility of inorganic things may be analogous: they also took their origin from the creator spirit, although they are not animated by that spirit intrinsically, as is true of the living beings. This throws a peculiar light on contemporary statements to the effect that modern physics does no longer offer a materialistic description of the universe. In commenting on the transition of physics from the concept of body to the field concept and to its attempts at explaining matter itself, Popper says, "Materialism transcends itself."[26] On the basis of similar arguments, the German physicist Georg Sübmann says, "The material of all things appears like a web out of thought."[27] This is not an idealistic statement. Rather, the spiritual dynamics in the natural processes makes it possible to understand how the human mind is able to grasp their structure and to make itself master of them.

Sübmann accepts that there is a correlation between spirit and life, if only one allows for a sufficiently broad concept of life. He distinguishes degrees of interiorization of the spiritual dynamics, starting not with plants and animals. Rather, he starts with physical streams and currents, then continues with the vegetative and sensitive life of plants and animals, before with the human spirit he comes to intellectual life.[28] But what can be taken as characteristic of a living entity as well as of the human mind, so that the capability of the mind to grasp the nature of things would be better understood?

One such characteristic seems to be bound up with the notion of *wholeness* or *gestalt*. Each living being is a *gestalt*, but it also perceives other things in terms of its form. There are primitive forms of gestalt perception, dependent on just a few abstract characters. They may be related to hereditary schemes of perception, and the occurrence of such perceptions may evoke equally hereditary responses. But particular gestalt perceptions may also be acquired by processes of learning, and the act of perception may go together with some more or less tacit awareness of the elements that are essential to that particular gestalt. Most forms of gestalt perception abstract from time, but there are also perceptions of living forms, which include their characteristic movement in time. It seems specific of living forms that time and movement are not accidental to the gestalt. The animal itself is such a living form, although not all animals seem able to perceive living forms as the human mind does. Human beings perceive not only animals as living forms, however, but also plants and even suborganic phenomena, like a flame—all apparently active and self-controlling systems. Moreover, living forms are open systems. For the perpetuation of their life they depend, as the fire does, on an environment, and at least animals have an intrinsic relation to the environment upon which they depend, and thus to time, to the future of their own lives, although they may not be aware of that future to which their drives are related. Time, thus, is intrinsic to the living form of an animal, but it also transcends its present structure. Life, therefore, is self-transcending, and as soon as an animal becomes aware, as the human mind does, of the temporal nature of a living form, it will also perceive the transcendence of time beyond its life and death.

It is interesting that the Hebrew language produced a word that precisely conceives of this self-transcendence and indigence of the living being. The word is *nefesh*,[29] and its connotations are largely lost when it is translated as "soul." Now precisely the *nefesh*, the living being in the process of its self-transcendence, is characterized in the biblical creation story as the special product of the spirit. The spirit, then, is related to form and wholeness, but more especially to the open system of the living form in the self-transcendent nature of its life process.

Do these considerations yield any result in view of our question for what the structure of a living being and the activity of the human mind may have in common, so that we may catch a glimpse of their common rooting in the spirit? First of all, the human mind perceives forms, unified wholes. But further, the analytic abilities of the mind allow for an awareness of wholes as integrating their parts and thus of living forms that progressively integrate the elements of their lives. The mind itself has often been characterized as an integrative activity, which is nourished, however, by its analytic capacity.[30] Kant was among the first to emphasize this synthetic and dynamic character of the mind's activity. It corresponds to the structure of the life process as an open system, but now that process of continuous and self-transcending integration takes place within the field of conscious awareness, which in the more primitive forms of perception seems to be limited to the abstract forms of the environment, while on the human level these forms are perceived as wholes of parts and therefore as constituent members of a situation, of a cosmos stretching out in space and time. The human person learns to perceive his or her own body and name as located within the cosmos of its social and natural world and to perceive his or her own life as a limited process in time, together with the question for a future beyond those limits, beyond the limits of death, and for the powers transcending the objects of world as forms of their appearance. It seems to be in this self-transcending integrative process that the human mind corresponds most closely to the dynamics of life and manifests its spiritual nature, sharing in a spiritual dynamics that transcends the individual mind itself. One aspect of such transcendence of the spiritual dynamics beyond the individual is expressed when one speaks of the spirit of a community: the forms of human community are the most obvious examples (though not the only ones) for processes of spiritual integration that transcend the life of the individual. On the other hand, although each individual human person participates in the spiritual dynamics, tensions and antagonisms develop within the community life and among its individual members. How does a pneumatological scheme of human reality account for that?

In the biblical tradition, as in other archaic cultures, one is confronted with the notion of evil spirits. How it may happen that a spiritual phenomenon turns evil becomes understandable on the basis of the integrative dynamics of spiritual processes. It is always a living form, organized around the center of self-transcendent activity and control that shares in spiritual dynamics. However, if its self-centeredness dominates its self-transcendent activity in such a way that it can no longer become a member of more comprehensive spiritual integrations, the drive toward self-transcendent integration itself becomes disruptive and divisive. Such a reflection offers a vantage point for a deeper appreciation of the early Christian differentiation between spirit and mind: although every living form shares in the life-giving breath of the divine spirit, no form of life as such is united to the dynamics of the spirit, because in its self-centeredness every living form may turn evil. This is true even of the human mind, although—or perhaps because—in the human mind the spiritual dynamics is interiorized to the highest degree. Therefore the human mind longs for full participation in the spirit that would satisfy our hunger for wholeness and disclose to us the nature of every creature. But the unambiguous satisfaction of such yearning is given to the mind not in the form of a definitive and exclusive possession, that the mind would inevitably surpass again, but only in the ecstasy of faith and of its hope, and in the creative love born from such faith.

Notes

1. Karl R. Popper and John C. Eccles, *The Self and Its Brain* (New York: Springer Verlag, 1977), 179f. "But how could the unextended soul exert anything like a push on an extended body?" (p. 180).
2. John Locke, *An Essay Concerning Human Understanding* (New York: Dover Publications, 1959), II, 23, 5.
3. David Hume, *A Treatise of Human Nature*, ed. L. A. Selby-Bigge, 2d ed. (1739/40; reprint eds.: Oxford: Clarendon Press; New York; Oxford University Press, 1978), 232ff., 250; cf. 251ff.
4. Cf. Popper and Eccles, *The Self and Its Brain*.
5. Ibid., 56ff.
6. Ibid., 22ff., esp. 27ff.
7. Ibid., 12f.
8. Ibid., 73 and 13; cf. 30ff.
9. Ibid., 109.
10. Ibid., 115; cf. 554ff.
11. Ibid., 437ff., esp. 441ff. Eccles is much more hesitant to attribute consciousness to animals, even to primates; cf. 518ff. and 534f.
12. Ibid., 38; cf. the remarks on language as a "tool," 48f.

13. Locke, *An Essay Concerning Human Understanding*, II, 23, 18, and 15.
14. Ibid., II, 23, 5.
15. Augustine, *De libero arbitrio*, 1.8.18: "Hoc quicquid est, quo pecoribus homo praeponitur, sive mens, sive spiritus, sive utrumque rectius appellatur. . . . Ratio ista ergo, vel mens, vel spiritus cum irrationalis animi motus regit, id silicet dominatur in homine cui dominatio lege debetur ea, quam aeternam esse comperimus." Cf. *De Trinitate* 14.16 (Corpus Christianorum, series Latina 50a, 453, 35ff.). Usually, Augustine prefers to speak of mind (*mens*) or of reason (*ratio*). That may be explained by the semantic complexity of the term "spirit" (see the diverse meanings enumerated in *De Genesi ad Litteram* 12.7f. and *De Trinitate* 14.16) or also by the danger of mistaking the term "spirit" for the divine spirit. To this, see *De Genesi contra Manicheos* 2.8 and also *De Genesi ad Litteram* 7.2ff. Perhaps it is not by accident that the anthropological discussions of his work on the Trinity do not refer to Gen. 2:7 except in the passing remark, 2.18.34.
16. Thomas Aquinas, *Summa theologiae* 1.97.3c: "Anima rationalis et anima est, et spiritus. Dicitur autem esse anima secundum illud quod est commune ipsi et aliis animabus, quod est vitam corpori dari . . . sed spiritus dicitur secundum illud quod est proprium ipsi, et non aliis animabus, quod silicet habet virtutem intellectivam immaterialem."
17. Ibid., 1.36.1c: "Nomen *spiritus* in rebus corporeis impulsionem quandam et motionem significare videtur; nam flatum et ventum spiritum nominamus." Cf. Augustine, *De Trinitate* 14.16 (Corpus Christianorum series Latina 50a, 452, 32ff.).
18. Immanuel Kant, *Anthropologie in pragmatischer Hinsicht* (1798), 57 (*Anthropology from a Pragmatic Point of View*, trans. Mary J. Gregor [The Hague: Nijhoff, 1974]); F. W. J. Schelling, "Ideen zu einer Philosophie der Natur" (1797), in *Werke*, ed. K. F. A. Schelling, 2, 51. Cf. Georg Marquardt, "Art. Geist," in *Historisches Wörterbuch der Philosophie* (1974), ed. J. Ritter, 3:184f., 186f. According to Marquardt, this romantic conception of Geist combines the aesthetics of genius and theology (pp. 187f.). For the post-Hegelian reduction of spirit to the individual consciousness, see pp. 199f.
19. Cf. Walther Zimmerli, *Ezekiel* (1969), 2:895; cf. 900 (*Ezekiel I*, trans. Ronald E. Clements, ed. Frank Moore Cross and Klaus Baltzer [Philadelphia: Fortress Press, 1979]). When Zimmerli (p. 895) distinguishes the conception of Ezekiel from Eccles. 12:7 in that in the word of the prophet the *ruach* does not come from God but is called from its presence in the world, this is a correct description of the vision itself (cf. Ezra 37:9), but Zimmerli's remark does not do full justice to the explanation, where the breath of life is explicitly related to the spirit of God himself (Ezra 37:14).
20. See Wolf-Dieter Hauschild, *Gottes Geist und der Mensch: Studien zur frühchristlichen Pneumatologie* (1972), 30ff., 36ff. (for Clement), 89ff. (Origen), 152ff. (Gnostics), 201ff. (Tatian), 206ff. (Irenaeus).
21. Ibid., 41f. (Clement).
22. According to E. Cassirer, *Philosophie der symbolischen Formen* (1923–29), 1:56f. (Eng. trans., *Philosophy of Symbolic Forms* [New Haven: Yale University Press, 1953–57]), this is characteristic of the mythical conception of language, while the differentiation of language from this

arises from the reflection that in language the object is only represented but not itself present (2:53).

23. Jean Piaget: *Nachahmung, Spiel und Traum* (1975), 116ff., 127ff., 310ff., 316ff.

24. Julian Jaynes in his presentation "The Evolution of Language in the Late Pleistocene" at the New York Congress on *Origins and Evolution of Language and Speech* (New York, 1976, 312–25, esp. 319) assumes a close interrelation of the origins of language, art, and religion. And Suzanne K. Langer conjectures that the festive celebrations of early cultic ritual may have provided the occasion for the first development of language (*Mind: An Essay on Human Feeling* [1972], 2:303ff., 307f.).

25. Karl Rosenkranz, *Der Ursprung der Sprache* (1961), 112f., 114ff. See the opposite argument in A. Montague, "Toolmaking, Hunting and Language," in *Origins and Evolution of Language and Speech*, 266–74.

26. Popper and Eccles, *The Self and Its Brain*, 1–35.

27. G. Süßmann, "Geist und Materie," in *Gott-Geist-Materie: Theologie und Naturwissenschaft im Gespräch*, ed. H. Dietzfelbinger and L. Mohaupt (Hamburg: Lutherisches Verlagshaus, 1980), 14–31, 20: "So erscheint uns der Stoff aller Dinge wie aus Gedanklichem gewirkt."

28. Ibid., 22f.

29. See Hans Walter Wolff, *Anthropologie des Alten Testaments* (1973), 25–40 (*Anthropology of the Old Testament*, trans. Margaret Kohl [Philadelphia: Fortress Press, 1974]).

30. Together with Karl Popper, John Eccles belongs to those who follow C. Sherrington in recognizing the decisive characteristic of the human mind in the integrative unity of consciousness (1.c.524; cf. Popper and Eccles, *The Self and Its Brain*, 127). But Eccles relates the integrative activity of mind directly to the vast plurality of neural cells, modules, and centers in the brain. From his insight that "the unity of conscious experience comes not from an ultimate synthesis in the neural machinery," he concludes that it must be placed "in the integrating action of the self-conscious mind on what it reads out of the immense diversity of neural activities in the liaison brain" (p. 356). According to Eccles, the mind selects from "the multitude of active centers at the highest level of brain activity" (p. 362) and "from moment to moment integrates its selection to give unity even to the most transient experiences" (ibid., cf. pp. 478, 488). But in fact the mind does not know of "brain events," except for a rather late stage of human research. The integrative activity of the mind is related to momentary perceptions and memories, not to brain events. The synthesis of brain events in the momentary perception ("a unified conscious experience of a global or Gestalt-character") is operating on another level than the integrative activity of the reflective mind. That Eccles—in contrast to Popper—does not properly distinguish between consciousness and self-consciousness (the self-conscious mind) becomes also evident in his dialogues with Popper on the origin of consciousness (cf. above, n. 11).

Index